"Essential reading for students and educators alike! Trainings in mindful presence are the hope for our next generation and for the healing of our world."
— Tara Brach, author of *Radical Acceptance* and *Radical Compassion*

"This beautifully structured, practical, and comprehensive book brings mindfulness to the college-aged population and the adults who work with them. Whether you are a young adult or an educator trying to introduce mindfulness into your classroom, this book is sure to serve as a thorough and relevant guide to the power of mindfulness practice."
— Diana Winston, director of Mindfulness Education at UCLA's Mindful Awareness Research Center and author of *The Little Book of Being*

"In this engaging and accessible approach to well-being, Linda Yaron Weston beautifully combines her expertise in mindfulness and education. She invites us into the present moment and captures the essence of mindfulness with fresh and interactive practices that build on one another. This is an important book for young adults who need a strong foundation to thrive. Highly recommended for students and the schools and organizations that serve them."
— Arianna Huffington, founder and CEO, Thrive Global

"Taking better care of ourselves, our families, and our communities is ever more critical for our nation's students, especially now. Linda Yaron Weston gives us fascinating insights into the science and practice of mindfulness with evidence-based lessons for teachers and students drawn from the neuro, social, physiological, and psychological sciences. This book makes the powerful case that mindful learning enables higher and deeper levels of students' academic and personal success, outcomes that we wish for each of our students."
— Dr. Martha J. Kanter, CEO of College Promise in Washington, DC and the former U.S. Under Secretary of Education for the Obama administration

"Linda Yaron Weston supplies us with a comprehensive program to help bring mindfulness to the classroom. In *Mindfulness for Young Adults,* she pairs mindfulness tools with day to day scenarios, offering students techniques to promote thriving in the classroom and in life. The course design provides avenues for deepening personal connections, maneuvering through emotions and supporting intellectual growth. This work will be of benefit to educational systems, teachers and students."

—Sharon Salzberg, author of *Real Happiness* and *Real Change*

"Linda Yaron Weston's work is an essential offering for the well-being of our young people and the health of our future. *Mindfulness for Young Adults: Tools to Thrive in School and Life* offers practical strategies in a comprehensive, interactive program to help calm the body, relax the nervous system, and create conditions for optimal healing, learning, and thriving. As our young people learn to care for themselves in this way, it does not only impact them—it impacts the health and well-being of our entire society. Thank you, Linda, for your expertise and passion."

—Jillian Pransky, author of *Deep Listening: Practices to Calm Your Body, Clear Your Mind, And Open Your Heart*

"This book taught me so many important lessons and techniques that have helped me learn and incorporate mindfulness into my everyday life. Cultivating mindfulness has shifted my mindset from one of fear and anxiety, to one of acceptance and gratitude. It has truly changed my life and has pushed me to evolve into a much more confident, compassionate, and positive person."

—Jacqueline Berliner, USC undergraduate class of '20

# Mindfulness for Young Adults

*Mindfulness for Young Adults: Tools to Thrive in School and Life* is an interactive experience designed to enhance mindful awareness and to aid in teaching and learning the principles and practice of mindfulness.

Blending theory, research, and practice to offer a comprehensive program for young adults to build well-being tools, each of the book's five modules includes engaging information, strategies, meditations, and activities designed to deepen understanding and application of mindfulness. It includes practical techniques to cope with emotions, work with thoughts, navigate stress, build resilience, make aligned choices, and be more present in life and relationships. In addition to the reflection and meditation activities found at the end of each module, the text also features a "resources" section complete with a mock exam, tips for course design, and resources for further study.

Designed for both students and teachers, this workbook can be used independently or in the classroom as either a textbook to an introductory mindfulness course or as a supplement for teaching well-being practices in any discipline.

**Linda Yaron Weston** teaches at the University of Southern California. Blending her expertise in mindfulness and education, she developed their introductory mindfulness course. She is a National Board Certified Teacher with a dual M.Ed.

# Mindfulness for Young Adults
## Tools to Thrive in School and Life

**Linda Yaron Weston**

Routledge
Taylor & Francis Group

NEW YORK AND LONDON

First published 2021
by Routledge
52 Vanderbilt Avenue, New York, NY 10017

and by Routledge
2 Park Square, Milton Park, Abingdon, Oxon, OX14 4RN

*Routledge is an imprint of the Taylor & Francis Group, an informa business*

*Library of Congress Cataloging-in-Publication Data*
Names: Yaron Weston, Linda, author.
Title: Mindfulness for young adults: tools to thrive in school and
life/Linda Yaron Weston.
Description: New York, NY: Routledge, 2021. | Includes bibliographical
references and index.
Identifiers: LCCN 2020031131 (print) | LCCN 2020031132 (ebook) |
ISBN 9780367615857 (hardback) | ISBN 9780367615833 (paperback) |
ISBN 9781003105626 (ebook)
Subjects: LCSH: Mindfulness-based cognitive therapy. |
Mindfulness (Psychology)
Classification: LCC RC489.M55 Y37 2021 (print) |
LCC RC489.M55 (ebook) | DDC 616.89/1425–dc23
LC record available at https://lccn.loc.gov/2020031131
LC ebook record available at https://lccn.loc.gov/2020031132

ISBN: 978-0-367-61585-7 (hbk)
ISBN: 978-0-367-61583-3 (pbk)
ISBN: 978-1-003-10562-6 (ebk)

Typeset in Times
by Deanta Global Publishing Services, Chennai, India

**For Dave**

**For Ima**

**For my students**

# Contents

# About the Author

*Photograph by Zvia Yaron, z"ll*

Linda Yaron Weston has the unique perspective of having taught both academic and well-being courses at the high school and university level. She lectures at the University of Southern California, where she developed and teaches the introductory mindfulness course. She holds dual M.Ed degrees from UCLA, B.A. degrees in human development and literatures of the world from UC San Diego, national board certification in English language arts, and California teaching credentials in physical education and health. She is certified in mindfulness facilitation through the UCLA's Mindful Awareness Research Center and is a certified yoga teacher (E-RYT 500) with specialty training in yoga therapy and restorative yoga. Her expertise in education, human development, meditation, yoga, and literature contribute to an integrative, interdisciplinary approach to mindfulness that blends theory, research, and practice. Through her career, she has worked to increase opportunities for students to thrive, particularly around the areas of mental and physical health, equity and access, and school and community partnerships. As a public high school English teacher, she designed and led real-world learning experiences, including a student art exhibition and presentation at the Department of Education in Washington, D.C. and a student photography exhibition on self-portraiture in partnership with The Getty Center and 826LA. She served as a U.S. Department of Education Teaching Ambassador Fellow as well as in the Fulbright Hays Seminars Abroad Program and U.S. State Department Teachers for Global Classrooms Program.

# Acknowledgments

In my mother's last days, she told me I should write a book. Thank you to my mom for believing in me and the selfless, wholehearted love that she gave to us all. And for my dad for showing such strength in love and resilience.

To the team at Routledge and especially my editor and editorial assistant, Amanda Devine and Grace McDonnell, for their encouraging support in helping this book come to be.

To my teachers who have been a light on the path with such wisdom and grace.

To USC PE and Steve VanKanegan for his visionary leadership and believing in me and mindfulness enough to let me develop the Introduction to Mindfulness course. To the awesome Amber Harris for being such a bright light of joy, support, and openness through it all. And to my mindfulness team, Amanda Gilbert and JoAnna Hardy, whom it is an honor to teach alongside.

To UCLA MARC's Diana Winston, for opening this beautiful door to being fully present and Marvin Belzer, whose incredible summer class I TA'ed inspired me to create one. Thank you for teaching me the richness of simplicity.

To my colleagues and dear friends who commented on this book as it was developing: Lisa Davis, whose inclusion of mindfulness at The Getty Villa has helped changed what it means for students to see art, Laura Loyola whose warmth and friendship has been a raft to me in life and work, and Clio Manuelian whose wholehearted living embodies the essence of mindfulness.

To my amazing students, who inspire and uplift me each day to be a better teacher and person because of their heart and courage. I would especially like to thank the students who contributed feedback and time for this book: Jacqueline Berliner, Scarlett Bress, Cristian Garcia, Megan Gates, Sahib Gill, Drew Hodis, Isha Khan, Agrima Kohli, Ari Semel, and Sudhakar Sood. To my student researchers who so diligently interviewed students in the course to capture their experiences: Shayla McPhearson, Cambria Peterson, and Sudhakar Sood. And to all those whose mindfulness journeys are shared here.

Most of all, thank you to my husband, Dave, whose kindness and love makes everything possible. You are my rock, my home, and my favorite writer of all time.

# Introduction

As an educator, it became increasingly clear to me that teaching well-being tools is just as important as academic skills. In order for my students to be able to fully focus on learning in the classroom, they needed tools for emotional regulation, stress resilience, coping with anxiety, dealing with grief, mental health supports, and learning to take a moment to pause and breathe and find stillness in the midst of it all.

Young adults are called on to face challenge after challenge in their personal, academic, and social lives. How do we show up to meet challenges? How do we hold the whole spectrum of life's joys alongside the difficulties? How do we make wise choices and live a life that is aligned with our values and intentions? How do we learn to be fully present in the moments of our lives and to live them well?

As what it means to live and learn evolves, it is essential for schools to examine what, why, and how they teach. This includes tools to navigate life alongside academics so that students can fully thrive. Offering well-being courses within the school day situates mental health support within students' academic experience. It provides comprehensive tools over a sustained period of time with peer group support, classroom accountability, and a safe space and common language to dialogue about challenges. It is a proactive approach that explicitly teaches well-being practices on the front end, rather than patchwork services after a tragedy has occurred or leaving it to chance that students will seek tools when needed.

The Introduction to Mindfulness course I developed with the mind-body branch of USC's Department of Physical Education seemed to fill a need for young adult mental and emotional supports. Through it, students learned practices to cope with emotions, work with thoughts, make aligned choices, and be more present in their lives and relationships. Each two-unit section that was offered quickly filled, as students began recommending the class to their roommates, partners, and friends. They told me they shared the workbook with their parents, attended meditation classes with their families, and had discussions with advisors about the impact mindfulness had on their lives. "If it was my school, I would make it mandatory because I know people run on such high stress all the time and being mindful isn't usually part of their daily discourse or conversation," remarked Mia, a junior majoring in cinema and media studies (unless otherwise noted, names have been changed to protect student privacy). She appreciated the opportunity to learn mindfulness in a class setting that offered a balance of accountability without being too academically demanding. "Having every student take this would be so helpful."

Mindfulness practices can be taught through an immersive course such as the one I teach, or through bringing practices into other content area classrooms or organizations that serve students. Since early in my career as a public high school English teacher in Los Angeles, I became increasingly passionate about how to correspondingly teach life coping skills alongside the academic subject. I sought to infuse my curriculum with resilience tools to support mental and emotional health—whether a few breaths to pause before starting class, studying themes of overcoming challenges, or leading after school yoga and meditation classes for students and faculty. It quickly became apparent that my students were not able to fully thrive in the classroom if they were overcome by anxiety or didn't have sufficient tools to navigate the life challenges they faced. This isn't to say that students don't already enter the classroom with a wealth of knowledge, capital, and resilience—or to individualize a systemic issue and remove responsibility from systems for fostering more equitable structures—but that offering supports amidst varying degrees of mental health challenges, backgrounds, and experiences can enhance personal tools to thrive on a collective level.

In the midst of the challenges that young adults face, it is my hope that more schools and universities structure mental health and well-being supports into the student academic experience. Just as science and English are seen as essential general education classes, so too can a well-being elective GE be structured into a student's academic experience. As a junior majoring in business, Devin had what he felt was his hardest semester the fall he signed up to take mindfulness. Yet, he flourished personally and academically as he learned well-being practices. He noticed that he made increasingly positive decisions, valued his friends and family more, built resilience to not give up when studying got difficult, and came to understand himself better. Mindfulness wasn't something he did on the side, but rather became a vehicle for positive transformation and resilience. "This is probably my roughest semester so far," he reflected in an interview about the course. "This class is like a weird gap in my really busy schedule today where I can just, it's like I'm doing something for myself instead of doing something for my GPA or someone else, so I think the class has been really beneficial to me."

Compiled from interviews and class written responses, Devin's reflections, and dozens of his peers are included throughout to provide voice to their process of learning to be more mindful, aware, and awake. This interactive book is primarily designed for use in an introductory mindfulness course or as a supplemental text to incorporate mindfulness practices into another course or program. It can also be used independently by young adults, organizations who serve them, families, and teachers. Each of the five modules includes practices, techniques, meditations, questions, and activities designed to deepen understanding and application of mindfulness. For depth and range of perspectives, student voices are placed alongside those in mindfulness, literature, psychology, and history. For broad accessibility, practices are discussed in a secular mindfulness framework. I do also here want to acknowledge the roots that mindfulness has in Buddhist philosophy and pay tribute to the teachers who have carried the practices through time and across continents. Though discussed in separate modules for organizational purposes, body, mind, and heart are interconnected. A thought can give rise to an emotion, and that sensation can be felt in the body. An emotion can trigger a thought. A gut instinct can be felt in the body before a thought or emotion is born. Mindfulness involves the union of this awareness, not the separation. Some things may apply more than others, so please take what works, modify to fit your unique circumstances, and leave the rest.

Well-being holds a worthy place in the discussion of what skills, knowledge, and dispositions help young adults to flourish, and who is responsible for teaching them. Mindfulness is not a silver bullet designed to save anyone. It is a field that offers tools to navigate experiences with awareness, acceptance, agency, curiosity, openness, and kindness. Imagine what a classroom and life would be like with greater amounts of those. That's one I hope to have and hope to share with my students.

# Module 1     Principles of Mindfulness

*There is a peace in the stillness.*

*A freedom available in each moment.*

*To arrive right here,*

*right now.*

*To feel the ground under our feet,*

*the sun on our skin.*

*To know that we are complete*

*and whole*

*just as we are.*

*To find home within this breath and this life.*

## 1.0  Introduction to Mindfulness

Mindfulness is something everyone can do and something that can be done anywhere, at any time, with no special equipment needed. The only thing you need is a willingness to be present with what you are experiencing. In many ways, writer and philosopher Henry David Thoreau sought mindfulness when he went to the woods to experience the realness that life had to offer. He writes in *Walden*:

> I went to the woods because I wished to live deliberately, to front only the essential facts of life, and see if I could not learn what it had to teach, and not, when I came to die, discover that I had not lived. I did not wish to live what was not life, living is so dear; nor did I wish to practice resignation, unless it was quite necessary. I wanted to live deep and suck out all the marrow of life, to live so sturdily and Spartan-like as to put to rout all that was not life, to cut a broad swath and shave close, to drive life into a corner, and reduce it to its lowest terms, and, if it proved to be mean, why then to get the whole and genuine meanness of it, and publish its meanness to the world; or if it were sublime, to know it by experience, and be able to give a true account of it in my next excursion.

Life is often so loud and busy that it becomes difficult to pay attention to what is really important. Or it's too painful to sit with ourselves in a challenging experience. We may spend life stuck thinking about the past or planning for the future and forget that life only happens in the present. Mindfulness can be a moment of stillness and presence in the chaos of daily life. A certainty of the present moment in all the uncertainty that exists. A reminder to live life fully by embracing the realness of it, in all of its joy, sorrow, and everything in between.

Tony was a junior majoring in neuroscience when he enrolled in Introduction to Mindfulness. He found that meditation offered him the realness that inspired Thoreau. "To me, mindfulness means chipping away at the chatter our minds create and experiencing life more fully," he reflected. He felt that rather than his attention preoccupied with whichever thoughts happened to arise, mindfulness helped him realize that he has the power to attend to his thoughts with consciousness. "This leads to a deeper understanding and appreciation for the present moment. It allows you to experience feelings and sensations previously hidden by the veil of thoughts and chatter. Overall, mindfulness to me means learning to live with passion."

Over time, we learn that we do not need to numb experiences or emotions with distraction. We learn to trust that we can let our thoughts and anxieties rest. We learn to send kindness to ourselves and others in the face of suffering in the human experience and create a little more freedom and spaciousness by doing so. With that freedom comes a choice in how we see our lives and the power to respond to events with awareness and presence rather than unconscious reactivity.

Mindfulness then becomes not just something we do when we're seated in meditation but a way of being in the world, with our eyes, minds, and hearts open to whatever arises. This takes courage and resilience, knowing that we will falter over and over, and yet we can come back to the breath, back to the body, back to the refuge of the moment. At the end of the day, that's all we have.

To begin, take a moment to pause. Inhale deeply. Exhale deeply. Experience this moment, right here, right now. Notice what is present and welcome it. Invitations to pause are included throughout. When you see one, take a moment to sense the ground under your feet, the breath moving through your body, and the experience of being present.

---

Pause for a moment and take a breath

**Reflect**

1.  What do you pay attention to most? To what extent do you choose what to pay attention to?

2.  Why might it be useful to develop the capacity to pay conscious attention?

3.  When do you feel like you're most present in life? Least present?

4.    In what situations might it be helpful to be less reactive and more responsive?

5.    Activity: if you know someone who meditates, interview them about why they do and how they began.

6.    Try it: decide an amount of time you can commit to meditating daily. Perhaps start with five minutes a day, or even one minute a day. It can be helpful to choose a time of day or place so that you can keep a consistent routine. Some might like to meditate first thing in the morning to start the day with stillness. Others might like to use it to decompress at the end of the day or as an afternoon pause. You can use a guided meditation or app. Find what works for you. Like any new skill, with time and practice, it will gradually deepen. Reflect on what you noticed.

## 1.1  What Is and Isn't Mindfulness?

*Preconceptions: True or False?*

1.  The goal of meditation is to clear our minds.
2.  Anyone can be mindful anywhere, anytime.
3.  Meditation has been shown to improve awareness, concentration, memory, brain function, and overall mental and physical well-being.
4.  Meditation has been shown to decrease inflammation and support telomeres.
5.  Mindfulness is a religion.
6.  Through mindfulness, we can learn tools to deal with and process difficult emotions.
7.  We can also learn to cultivate compassion and joy.
8.  Mindfulness is not a skill that grows with time and practice.
9.  Neuroplasticity has shown we can't change how the brain functions and can't rewire neuropathways.

*Explanations at end of section 1.2*

Mindfulness involves a willingness to be present with our experiences. It can be easy to unconsciously or automatically go through life on autopilot. We may want to numb the painful moments or keep ourselves busy to avoid sitting with discomfort. And yet, we have a choice in how we live our lives, how we show up for the big and little moments, and what we pay attention to.

Life is ultimately comprised of moments. We create our own reality of experience based on what we choose to focus on. Philosopher and early American psychologist William James observed, "My experience is what I agree to attend to." There are countless things that ask for the attention of young adults in this generation—from technology, social media, and advertisements, to friends, classes, families, television, music, politics, and so much more. Attention is a finite and precious resource that ultimately determines what life is about at that moment. We only have so much of it to give. Rather than giving attention by default to whatever asks for it, we can learn to live consciously and intentionally by choosing what we give our attention to based on what is important to us. When the world can be fast, loud, and demanding, mindfulness offers a moment of stillness in the midst of it all so that we can decide to slow down, tune in, get clear, and choose a response of freedom.

Mindfulness includes two elements:

1.  *What*: present-moment awareness of experiences
2.  *How*: with curiosity, acceptance, openness, and kindness

Mindfulness provides a choice to pay attention to each moment as it unfolds in front of and within us. It is a conscious, curious, and kind attention. Though it is possible to be aware of a moment with harsh judgment, mindfulness meets the moment with curiosity over judgment, acceptance over resistance, and kindness over harshness. Acceptance is not passive resignation. It is clearly seeing and knowing what is happening with open eyes. This clarity can invite a neutral discernment about how to wisely respond to experiences.

Mindfulness teacher Jon Kabat-Zinn defines mindfulness as "the awareness that emerges through paying attention on purpose, in the present moment, and nonjudgmentally to the unfolding of experience moment by moment." It takes courage to be willing to see clearly, to open into the full expression of life, and to sit with all that is present. "What mindfulness means to me is being fully in the present, no matter what thoughts, emotions, and experiences I have. It is about accepting and holding those difficulties with kindness and learning to not try to resist them," Jackson, a senior accounting major reflected. "Too many times, if I was having a difficult emotion or thought, I would try to force myself away and never quite address the situation for what it is. Through learning what mindfulness truly means, I have been able to be at peace with certain circumstances and finally heal."

Regardless of external definitions of mindfulness, it is up to each person to determine what mindfulness means to them. This can be done through clarifying why it might be useful and setting an intention of how best to show up to practice it. These answers will continue to evolve over time as mindfulness deepens.

---

Pause for a moment and take a breath

---

### Mindfulness Isn't

Mindfulness isn't about relaxing and going to an inner spa. Though relaxation and calm may occur as results of practice, mindfulness is more broadly about opening to the whole of the human experience, one moment at a time. Pema Chödrön writes in her book *How to Meditate*:

> We do not meditate in order to be comfortable…meditation gives us the opportunity to have an open, compassionate attentiveness to whatever is going on. The meditative space is like the big sky—spacious, vast enough to accommodate anything that arises.

Mindfulness is a courageous process that involves a willingness to welcome the spectrum of emotions without trying to resist, push away, or make things into what they aren't. When I first went on a weeklong meditation retreat, I thought it would be a relaxing vacation, but sitting with myself in all of my experiences with no distractions for a sustained period of time was some of the most confronting, difficult personal work I had done. When we sit with ourselves, we uncover what we've been holding onto and are called on to reconcile with what might be standing in the way of openness and freedom. In his book *After the Ecstasy, the Laundry*, Jack Kornfield writes:

> The journey is not about going into the light. The forces of our human history and entanglement are tenacious and powerful. The path to inner freedom requires passing through them. Receiving grace, opening to illumination, becoming wise has not been easy even for the masters. It is described as a difficult purification: cleansing, letting go, and stripping away. Suzuki Roshi called it a "general housecleaning of the mind." It is painful to cast off our own scales, and the dragons guarding the way are fierce.

It is not often easy work to begin, but it can lead to honest self-discovery as we sit with our bodies, hearts, and minds. To get to the other side involves passing through what has been standing in the way of freedom. Monica, a senior psychology major, initially thought mindfulness was a way to boost her mood. She came to realize that it gave her room to accept her emotions and experiences without forcing a response. "When I first began this class, mindfulness meant a quick way for me to feel good," she reflected. She ultimately found that while she may not always feel good, she now had room to accept her experience without forcing herself to feel a certain way. "This alone allows me to feel good in the not so good moments," she perceived. "Developing self-acceptance was something I never had, but I now understand a way to feel fully accepting of myself. In areas where I feel resistance, I no longer beat myself up over it. As a result, I can find a way to nurture my needs instead of suppressing the negative emotion."

Mindfulness isn't something that only certain people can do. Everyone can do it. All are included in a global community of practice that spans the spectrum of age, gender, sexual orientation, race, class, ethnicity, job, geographic location, past morality, and any other classification. For those who might be wondering if they can do it, or if it's for them—yes. You don't need to be calm or fit an image of what you think someone who meditates looks like. You can do it. It is for you. Just as you are right now in this moment.

Even more than something to do, it's a process of undoing the unconscious patterning and habits we've learned along the way. As children, we may have found it very easy to live in the moment, whether immersed in play or savoring an ice cream. We can relearn and rediscover what it feels like to live with beginner's eyes, without weighted armor, distraction, and scripted expectation.

This is not a passive practice. To be mindful isn't to be a pushover or to not work to make things better. On the contrary, mindfulness can cultivate wise thought and action through being able to more clearly see situations for what they are and respond from a space of wisdom rather than reactivity. How many times have we rashly reacted and wished we could have had a more patient and calm response instead? Regardless of how we were conditioned to respond to situations growing up, mindfulness is an invitation to choose a deliberate path that aligns with our values. Freedom comes when we can be in the midst of a charged situation, release its hook, take a breath, and pause to choose a conscious response.

Mindfulness isn't about clearing the mind. Humans are intellectual beings designed to think, reflect, and plan—and this has served a necessary evolutionary purpose. Thinking is not bad, and we don't need to stop thinking to be mindful. Through mindfulness, we can learn to skillfully work with thoughts, emotions, body sensations, and our relationship to experiences so that we can be more present with what is happening when it is happening. Many people may think they can't meditate because their minds are too busy, though this is exactly a reason to consider meditating. When one begins practicing, it can be surprising how loud and frequent thoughts are. It can seem like thoughts are coming even more frequently, but it is simply that we are now noticing what has been happening unconsciously all along. At this point, we can decide if we are a slave to our thoughts, if we stay caught in our storylines, or if we learn to find the freedom to guide our attention in more skillful ways.

Classes in math, English, science, and history are commonly taken throughout one's education, and it isn't often that one may take a class that teaches how to work with thoughts, process emotions, and direct attention to the present so that we can choose to live consciously. Yet, we can learn how to do this just as we would learn skills in any other field of study. In her book *Grit: The Power and Passion of Perseverance*, Angela Duckworth proposes the equation:

$$\text{Skill} \times \text{Effort} = \text{Achievement}$$

Notably, various elements may complicate the seeming neatness of Duckworth's equation, including mental health challenges and social inequality. And while some may seem to have more of a tendency to live in the moment and process emotions and thoughts, through a growth mindset, we can all learn to cultivate this capacity with practice. Psychologist Carol Dweck's research on fixed versus growth mindsets found that it is more beneficial to focus on how we can learn and grow rather than thinking that we are either good or bad at something. Applied to mindfulness, through practice, we can learn to get better and grow our capacity to be present in the moments of our lives. Research in neuroplasticity reveals the brain's continued, flexible capacity to change and rewire neuropathways based on what we practice. We can grow new pathways to respond to experiences the more we practice presence and awareness.

Mindfulness will naturally strengthen over time and is not something that needs to be strived for or achieved in a traditional sense. Though learning is often transactional in outcomes and results, mindfulness asks us to trust in the process of the journey without getting too caught up in what it will do for us. In the eagerness to get to the next stage in life, or graduate, or find a job, with mindfulness, we can learn to savor each phase. Writer and philosopher Alfred D'Souza is credited with the quote:

> For a long time it had seemed to me that life was about to begin—real life. But there was always some obstacle in the way. Something to be got through first, some unfinished business, time still to be served, a debt to be paid. Then life would begin. At last it dawned on me that these obstacles were my life.

When we pay attention to life as it unfolds, we can be present in all of our moments and realize this is life happening right now. With that, we can choose how we show up for it.

**Reflect**

1.   What does mindfulness mean to you?

2.   What do you think is the opposite of mindfulness?

3.   What might get in the way of being mindful?

4.  What does it mean to mediate as someone who identifies as _____ (choose an identification you hold—gender, race, ethnicity, sexuality, age, location, etc.).

5.  Activity: find an article about mindfulness. Write a reflection that includes a summary of the article, your takeaways, how it might apply to your or your peers, and any lingering questions you may have.

6.  What do you think it would take to increase your capacity to be even more present? How might this enhance your life?

## 1.2 Why Mindfulness? The Science and Benefits

The 1946 preamble to the constitution of the World Health Organization describes health as a "state of complete physical, mental, and social well-being and not merely the absence of disease or infirmity." This is an interconnected mind-body approach to health. Through mindfulness, Devin gained agency to enhance all three elements of his physical, mental, and social well-being. "This course has greatly helped me see large improvements in myself. I make better decisions, learn from my mistakes and have made great life changes," he reflected. "I have almost completely given up drinking and find solace more in exercise and productive activities than destructive ones. I value my friends and family more and am extremely satisfied with where I am in life and where I am going." He declared, "I am extremely proud of myself for how far I have come."

Though the research is still young and emerging, mindfulness has been shown to contribute to well-being across all three components of health. A brief overview of selected research is included here.

### *Mental*

Neuroplasticity refers to the brain's capacity to change. Studies using brain scan imaging have shown that both structure and function of the brain are enhanced in positive ways with meditation. One such study showed that eight weeks of meditation practice led to brain changes in gray matter concentration, which appeared in parts of the brain responsible for learning and memory, emotion regulation, and perspective taking. Brain scans have shown that long time meditators did not experience the same type of cortical thinning with age as non-meditators. Mindfulness has also been shown to improve attention, concentration, and clarity. It can broaden the scope of our focus, leading to deeper creativity and problem-solving.

Mindfulness can aid in emotional regulation and navigating difficult emotions like stress and anxiety. In brain scans of meditators compared to nonmeditators, the prefrontal cortex region (considered the CEO of the brain responsible for decision making) was found to be enhanced, while the amygdala region of the brain (known as the brain's alarm center) had lower activity. This has implications for how experiences are processed and how we can learn over time to develop more responsiveness and less reactivity in times of stress.

Being happy also appears to be enhanced by being present. In a Harvard study by Matthew Killingsworth and Dan Gilbert, 2,250 people were asked multiple times a day for weeks on their phone what they were doing and how present they felt. The study found that people spent only about fifty percent of their time in the present moment, and they were less happy when their minds were wandering, no matter where they were or what they were doing.

### *Physical*

Physiologically, mindfulness has been shown to improve the immune system, increase quality of sleep, and decrease inflammation. Mindfulness can provide a pathway to calm the nervous system and has been shown to support the body down to the cellular level by delaying the shortening of telomeres, the protective sheaths at the ends of each chromosome which fray with age and stress.

The field of psychoneuroimmunology explores the impact of attitudes, beliefs, emotions, and mental state on the immune system. The mind and body are in constant dialogue and interaction. In one study, participants were infected with the rhinovirus (the common cold) and quarantined for six days. Those who were found to have high positive emotions got fewer colds. This is not to say that we need to push away difficult experiences to stay healthy, but mindfulness practices can be used to examine our relationship to emotions and to process our experiences, which then can support our integrated body systems.

Epigenetics is the study of gene expression. While we may have the genetic disposition for certain conditions, whether that condition manifests may depend, to some extent, on dynamic factors including genetics, environment, stress, nutrition, and lifestyle. Some genes may never get turned on. To a certain extent, mindfulness can be a protective health factor through calming the nervous system and developing resilient responses to stress that can support our genes.

### *Social*

Mindfulness also seems to enhance kindness and altruism. In a study that evaluated whether or not people would offer their chair to someone on crutches in a waiting room, 50% of the people who practiced mindfulness beforehand gave up their chair, compared to 15% of the people who didn't.

Relational mindfulness practices can increase active listening, as we turn to see one another with presence and openness. Mindfulness has been shown to reduce implicit age and race bias. This can have implications for how we relate to one another in casual, educational, and professional settings. Nicole, a senior majoring in sociology, remarked that she had become a "better friend, daughter, and sibling" as a result of mindfulness. A senior economics major, Charlie, recounted that after applying mindfulness in his communication with family members, his mother jokingly asked him, "Who are you, and what did you do with my son?"

Though mindfulness has been shown to have many benefits, it is not a cure-all panacea. It is not a savior. It is not a replacement for therapy or modern medicine. What it can be is a powerful complement to building healthier mind-body awareness and function so that unconscious patterning can give way to living a life that is more present, awake, and aware.

---

Pause for a moment and take a breath

---

### Why Practice?

Mindfulness is a moment of stillness from the loud and fast inner and outer worlds. We can relax into the moment and show up with acceptance for exactly what it is, exactly as we are. It provides the opportunity to see what is happening in our lives and in the world more clearly. It allows a space to step back from the stories we tell ourselves and find truth in the spacious awareness of witnessing our experience without getting lost in it. With this clarity, we can listen deeply to our inner wisdom and access a vast depth of knowledge that comes from clear seeing and tuning in.

Mindfulness is a way of living and interacting with the world around and within us. It allows us to determine how we want to live our lives and what we want them to mean. In his book, *A Path with Heart*, Jack Kornfield writes:

> In the stress and complexity of our lives, we may forget our deepest intentions. But when people come to the end of their life and look back, the questions that they most often ask are not usually, "how much is in my bank account?" or "how many books did I write?" or "what did I build?" or the like. If you have the privilege of being with a person who is aware at the time of his or her death, you find the questions such a person asks are very simple: did I love well, did I live fully, did I learn to let go?

Mindfulness enables the discovery of these questions and the choice of how to live. Much of life is spent reflecting on the past or thinking of the future. Mindfulness provides another alternative of living in intimate contact with direct experiences with responsive attentiveness to what is happening when it is happening. With this comes an uncovering of who we are and what kind of lives we want to live. In his book *Full Catastrophe Living*, Jon Kabat-Zinn writes:

> When it comes right down to it, the challenge of mindfulness is to realize that "This is it." Right now is my life. This realization immediately gives rise to a number of vital questions: "What is my relationship to my own life going to be? Does my life just automatically 'happen' to me? Am I a total prisoner of my circumstances or my obligations, my body or my illness or my past, or even of my to-do lists? Do I become hostile, defensive, or depressed if certain buttons get pushed, happy if other buttons are pushed, and anxious or frightened if something else happens? What are my choices? Do I have any options?"

Mindfulness affords options for how to show up in life. Life then doesn't just happen to us; it happens with awareness and intention to shape our responses and purposefully choose the life we will live. It is up to each person to find their own reason for practicing. "Mindfulness is so many things to me," reflected Vivian, a senior theatre major. "In one way, it's a tool I use to control, allow, and accept my thoughts and feelings in a healthy and insightful manner. Another use of mindfulness is its influence as a lifestyle, and how I use my practice towards self-growth and living a life of kindness, curiosity, and empathy for others," she observed.

"Using mindfulness as a tool in my back pocket, and as a goal for a lifestyle I want to live by, has benefited my physical, mental, and spiritual well-being for the better to a great extent."

As we sit in meditation, we learn to develop a trust in the process and practice of letting go, of opening to the experience, of softening our hearts with acceptance and nonjudgment for what emerges. Jack Kornfield goes on to write in *A Path with Heart*:

> To take the one seat requires trust. We learn to trust that what needs to open within us will do so, in just the right fashion. In fact, our body, heart, and spirit know how to give birth, to open naturally, like the petals of a flower. We need not tear at the petals nor force the flower. We must simply stay planted and present.

We can release focus on the result of getting somewhere and trust that the process and practice will unfold in exactly the way we need it to. Freedom emerges from the choice that mindfulness provides. We learn that we can consciously choose our response to life and show up from a place of awareness and wisdom. Mindfulness offers clarity and understanding to wisely respond to life, rather than unconsciously reacting by default or patterning. This is the freedom to choose how we live.

---

*Preconceptions Explained*

1. F—Mindfulness involves the willingness to be present in our experiences and hold them with kindness, curiosity, acceptance, and nonjudgment. It isn't about clearing the mind as much as holding space for what arises and consciously directing awareness to the present.

2. T—Mindfulness can be practiced by anyone, anywhere, at any time.

3, 4. T—Mindfulness has been shown to have various benefits for mental, physical, and social well-being.

5. F—Mindfulness has roots in Buddhism similar to the way that yoga has roots in Hinduism. Both have since been adapted to modern, Western practices and application of them can span the spectrum from secular to spiritual. For broad accessibility, mindfulness is discussed here in a secular framework. The willingness to pause and be present in our lives is a philosophy, not a religion.

6, 7. T—Mindfulness practices include techniques for working with emotions.

8. F—Just like learning a language or sport, with time and practice, we can enhance our capacity to be more present.

9. F—The brain can change throughout our lives. With mindfulness, we can replace deep grooves of unconscious patterning with new ways of seeing the world.

**Reflect**

1.  What is your reason to practice mindfulness?

2.  What misconceptions might there be about mindfulness? Where do you think they came from?

3.  How might health disparities in physical, mental, and social well-being impact different populations? What are the causes and conditions of these disparities?

4. Activity: find an article or research study about the science of meditation. Reflect on your takeaways and the implications of how it might relate to you or others. What lingering questions does it leave unanswered?

5. How is your meditation practice going? What have you noticed? What is most interesting or challenging about it?

## 1.3  How To: Foundations and Obstacles in Practice

Everyone has the capacity to meditate. You don't need any special tools or to be anything or anywhere other than what and where you are. What it takes is a willingness to pay attention to what's happening in this moment and be with it. In this lies both its simplicity and complexity.

### Time

*When*: choose a time of day—whether morning, afternoon, or evening, and commit to it. Each person has their own internal time clock and it may take some experimenting to find what works for you. Many prefer to start the day with a few moments to pause and center. Others may want to have time at the end of the day to decompress and unwind before bed. Some may want a midday reset. Some may find they are too sleepy for meditation in the mornings, and others may find evening mediation puts them to sleep. Find what works for you. Perhaps attach meditation to an existing ritual, like before breakfast or after an evening shower.

*How long*: you may want to set a designated amount of time so that you can relax into your meditation without having to determine if you should stay more or less time. Try not to get too hung up on the minutes. For starting out, try five minutes, or even one minute—one breath at a time. A little bit every day is better than a large amount infrequently. I keep a watch next to me. Some use an alarm on their phone; others may use an app timer. Just like a car takes time to slow before coming to a stop, I do find that it takes a bit of time for the mind to settle into practice, and that staying longer is more beneficial to me than if I were to end before arriving. If you miss a day or period of time, approach it with gentle kindness and try again next time.

### Place

If you can, choose a peaceful place to practice and create your own meditation space. It doesn't have to be fancy or large; just a floor cushion or chair is sufficient. Conditions don't need to be ideal. Just where we are, as we are, is enough. Arrange your space so that it feels meaningful and purposeful for you. Sitting practice is the most traditional form, though if that is not accessible, try standing meditation or walking meditation. Again, find what works for you.

### Seated Posture

Meditation posture has a nobility and dignity. It isn't rigid, and it isn't effortless. Sit upright with the crown of the head towards the ceiling or sky—with a balance of effort and ease. Sit on a cushion or in a chair. If you are sitting in a chair, adjust the height of your seat so that your thighs are parallel to the floor. This can be done with a blanket, towel, or cushion on the seat or under your feet. If you are sitting cross-legged, place a cushion or neatly folded towel or blanket underneath you so that your knees can be in line with, or slightly lower than, your hips. Over time, back muscles will strengthen, and you will be able to sustain a comfortable seat for a longer period of time. Meanwhile, you can sit with your back against a wall if needed.

Note: In the yoga tradition, it is common to begin with movement (asanas), then lying down (savasana) before beginning formal seated breath meditation (pranayama) practice. This helps to discharge energy and calm the body to prepare for sitting. Though this isn't traditional for mindfulness practice, I've found it can be helpful for preparing the body for seated meditation practice.

When beginning a new endeavor, it is common to develop goals and strive to meet them. There is a transactional expectation that if we put effort in, we will achieve a certain result. And yet, something different is called for in mindfulness—an intentional commitment to practice, rather than a striving goal based on an expected result. Ali, a freshman majoring in business, had heard of the benefits of meditation and started out thinking it would get him those things. He came to find that it was when he let go of the results and focused on his practice that he could experience the benefits. "At first, my goal from meditating was to gain all the benefits it promised, such as less stress and more freedom, but I soon realized that as long as I meditated for the sole reason of healing, I will never heal," he reflected. Over time, he came to realize that it was only when he let go of his need for benefits that he began to notice greater clarity and stillness. "It allowed me to see and accept the world just as it is and not always as I want it to be. I have become more able to deal with difficult emotions in a way that I do not identify with them, which has really allowed me to better manage them, and I would say that I am a much more mature person mentally than I was."

There is a wise type and amount of effort that gives rise to a quality of concentration in practice. It isn't passive, yet it isn't forceful. The balance is found in a middle way that is bold, yet relaxed. Here, we can hold the regal nature of body and mind and at the same time soften into it. We don't need to overly strive. Paying attention for just one breath at a time can cultivate the capacity for concentration. Joseph Goldstein writes in his book *Insight Meditation*:

> It is important not to become overly ambitious. We all have the capacity to feel one breath completely. But if we try to do more than that, if we have the idea that we are going to be mindful of our breathing for half an hour, then that is much too much. To sustain unbroken attention for that amount of time is far beyond the capacity of our mind, and so we quickly become discouraged. Connect and sustain for just one breath…and then one more. In this way you can work well within your capacity, and your mind will begin to concentrate simply and easily.

When sitting, listen to the tone of voice that arises. Is it kind or harsh, curious or judging, friendly or combative? Sometimes alternating and sometimes multiple ones at the same time. With awareness, we can soften and hold any harsh tones with patience and gentleness. If they come, we may even say to ourselves, "Can I hold this too with kindness?" Rather than judging or personally identifying with the tone, we can note it and accept our whole selves, exactly as they are.

### STOP Technique

STOP provides an opportunity to tune in to what is present and notice how we are relating to the moment. In the momentum of the day, we can pause, notice what arises, take a breath, and choose a response.

Stop and pause
Take a breath
Observe what is present and notice how the experience feels in your body
Proceed to make an intention or choice of what to do or how to show up next

Taylor, a sophomore majoring in business, found that STOP was helpful for her to pause and notice what she was holding. She reflected, "I can tend to overreact, especially to negative emotions. Strategies like the STOP technique have really helped me pause and think about how I truly feel about a situation." Pausing when she was in the midst of a charged experience provided space to decide how she wanted to show up in the moments after.

| |
|---|
| Pause for a moment and take a breath |

### Directed Awareness

It is natural for the mind to wander, whether reflecting on the past, planning for the future, or getting lost in a storyline. Directing attention to an anchor or home base gives the mind something to land on. When a sound, thought, or body sensation inevitably pulls attention away from the present, we can direct focus back to the anchor. The mind will wander, again and again, and we gently and patiently bring it back each time. After a while, we begin to catch ourselves sooner and are able to more easily come back home. Rather than harshly judging the mind for wandering, we can celebrate the moments of noticing and then bring the attention back. The noticing is the mindfulness. Just like any kind of training, it takes time and effort to cultivate the quality of concentration in your meditation practice, so try to be patient and kind when learning this new skill.

In choosing an anchor, it can be helpful to start with a directed, single point like the breath, body, or sound. You might bring one to the foreground of attention and let the others rest in the background of awareness. Experiment to find what works for you. For some, it may be comfortable to focus internally on the breath or body, and for others, it may feel better to start with a neutral, external focus like sound. Whatever your anchor, and however directed or spacious it may be, hold it lightly, without rigidity or grasping. Allow it to rest in your awareness and keep gently directing attention back to it each time the mind wanders.

### Breath

Each breath is an invitation to arrive in the present moment. Follow the breath as it moves in and out of your body. Observe it traveling through the nose, down the throat, and how it changes the shape of your spine and gently guides your abdomen with each breath. Perhaps pick a place that the breath is felt and use that location as an anchor, like the base of your nostrils or the bottom of your front ribs. Or you can choose a part of the breath—the very beginning of the breath, the end of the breath, or the slight pause when the breath is suspended at the end of one before the start of another. The important thing here is not to do anything with force, or even effort. You can cultivate a relaxed quality where you are simply an observer or witness of the breath, noticing its movement as it breathes you. Notice the length of the breath, the width of the breath, and the depth of the breath as it fills your front, back, and side body. Notice the abdomen recede to the spine with each exhale.

### Body

Notice your body in the space it's in and how it is supported by the surface underneath you. Sense your feet on the floor, rooted and secure. Either stay sensing your feet on the floor and the sensations it brings, or scan your body, from the crown of your head to the soles of your feet, noticing the sensations of each part (head, torso, arms, legs). It may be soothing to place a palm on the abdomen or chest to notice the gentle rise and fall of the breath and hold space with gentle, physical touch on the body.

### Sound

Sometimes when outside sounds arise as we meditate, we may want to push them away in the hopes of perfectly silent meditation conditions. However, we aren't trying to create perfect conditions as much as we are training ourselves to open to what is present in our experience. We can train our minds to notice sound—without trying to resist, push away, or make it into anything other than what it is. We can also notice ambient sounds, like the hum of the air conditioner, the tick of the clock, or louder sounds that pull our attention. Can we stay with this too? We may explore sound progression of the very start of the sound, the end of a sound, the middle of the sound before it ends, or the space between sounds. Or we can explore the nearest or farthest sound. We may notice the texture of the sound. Is it soft or sharp, smooth or rough, does it have a color, speed, or temperature? Perhaps we can even get still enough to sense our own internal sounds, like the breath or heartbeat. And we may here too notice our relationship to the sound itself.

### Open Awareness

In contrast to the directed awareness of concentrating on a single anchor, in open awareness, attention expands to include whatever is present in your experience. It is a natural, boundless, choiceless awareness rather than directed to a single point. It is the awareness of the awareness. It opens to include all experiences, sensations, thoughts, emotions, or whatever arises. In open awareness, everything can just pass by and through without the mind getting stuck on any of it. It isn't a struggle, striving, or making happen. It is a being, rather than a doing.

> Pause for a moment and take a breath

### Obstacles in Practice

There are many things that may get in the way of practice. Seeming hindrances can become our greatest teachers, as we begin to notice when they appear and what our response is to them. We can nonjudgmentally notice them and send kindness and patience to ourselves as we explore our response and relationship to them. Pema Chödrön writes in her book *How to Meditate*:

> The place of meeting our edge, of accepting the present moment and the unknown, is a very powerful place for the person who wishes to awaken and open their heart and mind. The present moment is the generative fire of our meditation. It is what propels us toward transformation. In other words, the present moment is the fuel for your personal journey. Meditation helps you to meet your edge; it's where you actually come up against it and you start to lose it. Meeting the unknown of the moment allows you to live your life and to enter your relationships and commitments ever more fully. This is living wholeheartedly.

The test of mindfulness is how we meet what arises, not just when things are lovely, but when we are sitting in the fire of life. How do we meet uncertainty, discomfort, pain, and fear? It is our relationship to the spectrum of experience that determines our response and freedom.

### Attachment and Aversion

As humans, we are programed to seek pleasure and avoid pain. We may notice wanting to hang onto what we have or push away what we don't want. Try to notice when attachment or aversion arise, see the resistance that might be present, hold it with kindness, notice how it feels, and gently return attention back to the breath, anchor, and present moment. We don't need to forcefully resist the attachment or aversion, we are simply noticing and perhaps loosening their grip by getting a little space around them.

*Doubt*

We may doubt our ability to practice or sustain our practice. We doubt ourselves, the practice, or our teachers. Who are we to do this work? Do we have what it takes to keep going? If things haven't worked in the past, who's to say that they will now? Doubt attempts to claw away at the trust and confidence of practice and leaves us second guessing our ability to withstand. We have options in how we approach it. When doubt sets in, we can take a breath, notice it's there, and try not to get too attached or identify with it personally. We can choose trust over doubt. We don't have to have all the answers. We can trust in our practice and community of practitioners to hold us up when it feels like we can't support ourselves. We don't have to hold confidence that we can do something forever. We just need enough for the next moment of breath, and the next. We can return to our motivation of why we are choosing to practice and hold kindness and space for whatever may arise.

A senior majoring in journalism, Lucia entered the mindfulness course thinking that she wasn't good at meditating and that it wouldn't be much use to her. "I came in with the preconceived idea that I wasn't good at it, and it wasn't for me. I had expectations of what my practice should look like and how I should be feeling each time," she reflected. Lucia initially thought there wouldn't be much growth. "All of my assumptions were incorrect. Meditating has been a form of therapy for me. I have asked myself questions I never have before and started to look at life in a different way. I have noticed many positive changes in my life because of mindfulness and meditation."

*Sleepiness*

Typically, when we are very relaxed we are asleep. In meditation, we are training our minds and bodies to be relaxed, yet alert. There may be a subtle initial resistance to being present with certain moments of our lives and sleepiness may emerge as a response to it. Our minds may fog over when we try to sit with awareness. When this happens, we can modify our practice so it can meet us where we're at. Over time, we can learn how to be relaxed and awake. We can try standing meditation, walking meditation, or moving meditation. We can notice what times of the day sleepiness is greatest and try to practice at alternate times. If practicing in the evening before bed is too tiring, try first thing in the morning, or on a break in the day. We can modify our practice so that we're meditating at multiple times of the day for shorter increments rather than in one big chunk. Find what works for you and bring kind attention to whatever arises.

*Restlessness*

It can be confronting to sit with our human experience. We might feel an itch, or the need to move positions. Our minds may feel fast and restless. Emotions can be uncomfortable to sit with. When we are still, we notice what is within and it may make us want to do something, anything, to quell the discomfort. It might be necessary to pause practicing if there is pain, trauma, or overwhelm. Otherwise, if possible, try to stay with it, notice it, be with it, hold it with patience and gentleness. This can give rise to the confidence that whatever comes our way, we can build the inner resources to weather any storm. If needed, modify practice or try walking meditation or mindful movement before sitting. A senior majoring in biology, Frank found walking meditation to be helpful for restlessness through anchoring his attention in movement of the body. "The walking meditation, especially, spoke to me as I am an active and often restless person," he reflected. "I was fully drawn in by this practice, not only because it anchored my oft wandering mind, but also because it satisfied my body's need to move. By thinking each step through, every muscle movement and every breath, I was able to truly engage in my practice."

## Reflect

1. What attitude do you generally approach tasks with?

2. What does it mean for you to have a balanced attitude and effort in practice?

3. To what extent, or where, do attachment and aversion appear in your life? What do you do in the face of them?

4.    To what extent, or when, has doubt appeared in your life? What do you do in the face of it?

5.    Try it: choose an anchor of body, breath, sound. Meditate with it for a few minutes. Place your attention on that anchor. When the mind wanders, gently bring it back. Without trying to make the experience anything other than what it is, just notice what comes up for you. Reflect on your experience.

## 1.4  School and Community Lens: Mindful Learning

Students may enter the classroom with stressors and challenges that impact their capacity to learn. Through awareness practices, we can learn to bring curiosity, presence, and attention to learning. Mindfulness can help students get centered and present to engage with the academic content. When they reflect on their relationship to what they're learning, they become active participants in the process through their interaction with the material. This can be applied across disciplines, as students examine what it means to be fully present in learning.

### *Students: Principles of Mindful Learning*

1.  *Curiosity.* Approach learning with curiosity and a willingness to explore, create, and interact with the content.
2.  *Intention.* Set an intention for how you will show up for learning and why it's important to you. This can even be one word that you keep coming back to—try, open, process, goal.
3.  *Attention.* When the mind wanders, try to bring the attention back to the content, conversation, or activity and not get swept away by a thought, emotion, or sensation. Notice what arises, then gently bring the attention back to the anchor. Put away anything that may distract or fragment attention. Only have out what is needed.
4.  *Single-tasking.* Multitasking splits attention between various things. In a classroom, students may be half listening to a lecture as they browse online, chat with a friend, or prepare for a future class. This can leave attention disjointed and fragmented. Single-tasking means we do only one thing at a time, and we bring our full attention to that activity. This makes it more possible to focus on the content and have more thoughtful ideas and participation.
5.  *Beginner's mind.* Even if school is a daily and repeated activity, can we approach each experience as if for the first time?
6.  *Creativity.* Mindful breathing, pauses, and emotional regulation can lower the stress response and help broaden the mind to think more creatively and critically.
7.  *Pausing to absorb.* Take pauses and STOP (Stop, Take a Breath, Observe, Proceed) to observe and absorb the material. Manage the intake of content and output of interaction through pauses.
8.  *Active speaking and listening.* Build listening skills by bringing full attention to the communication taken in (listening to another, the words on a page, or any content absorbed through the senses). Also, be intentional of what is put out (words, projects, actions, movement). Pause before speaking to develop a thoughtful response.
9.  *Connection.* Listen with nonjudgmental attention to build connection, safety, and trust in discussions. Cooperative group opportunities can deepen relationships and social support.

10. *Responsive vs reactive.* When situations arise, take a breath and choose a response rather than unconsciously acting out. Before going into triggering situations, think of what you might say or do in advance.

11. *Managing emotions.* Notice what emotions may arise in learning, whether frustration in learning difficult content, excitement in learning something new, anxiety before an exam, uncertainty in grades, wondering about fitting in, or joy in working with friends. Label and allow emotions rather than pushing them away, investigate how they feel in the body, and try not to identify with them as part of your personality. Hold what arises with kindness.

12. *Kindness and compassion.* When difficulties arise, choose to meet them with kindness. Try to hold your challenges, and the challenges of others, with compassion and nonjudgment, realizing we all make mistakes, and we are all learners in this world.

---

Pause for a moment and take a breath

---

### *Teachers: Incorporating Mindfulness in the Classroom*

1. Take a few moments to pause and breathe when coming together. This creates a separation from what happened before everyone got there. Younger students may respond to more tactile direction—a snap after three deep breaths, or hand movements to visualizing following the breath moving through the body like an elevator.

2. Create shared norms of classroom learning so that each student verbalizes what they need in a class environment so that they can best learn.

3. Articulate growth mindset principles for learning. The thing we practice is the thing that grows.

4. Hold space so that all students feel seen, heard, understood, and valued in discussion.

5. Set and reinforce boundaries around items that may get in the way of learning.

6. Explicitly teach how to redirect attention and focus when thoughts or distractions arise.

7. Dialogue about how to manage difficult emotions around performance tasks, such as anxiety before an exam or presentation.

8. Discuss how to navigate frustrations around learning difficult material.

9. Use mindful walking to observe surroundings and sense how the body moves through space with each step.

10. Teach the STOP Technique (Stop, Take a Breath, Observe, Proceed) when learning material or observing content. Use senses to notice sights and sounds, or tune in to notice any present body sensations, emotions, or thoughts that arise.

11. Structure activities that build connection and relationships in cooperative groupwork.

12. Model and practice active speaking and listening strategies. Activity example: in pairs, one person asks the other a repeated question like, "What do you notice?" This could be in response to visual or written content. After the response, they will say "thank you." This is repeated for a specific duration (1-3 minutes) and then the roles switch. The listener tries to bring full attention to the person and words listened to. The speaker tries to speak authentically from the heart. Both also try to stay connected to their own bodies. This activity invites participants to deeply look and uncover what's below surface answers. The repetition allows for curiosity and exploration, knowing what is expected and that there are no incorrect answers or prior knowledge needed to participate in discussions. Though it may seem unnatural to reply with a simple "thank you" for an answer, and we may be prone to validate, respond, or ask follow-up questions, it gives students language to dialogue and is simply an acknowledgment of their sharing that safely allows students to contribute without feeling there is a right or wrong answer.

### Impact of Mindfulness on Learning

Explicit instruction of mindfulness practices for working with thoughts and emotions was found to help students not only enhance their own well-being but also better access the academic content they were learning across classes. In a survey at the end of the Fall 2019 semester, over two-thirds of students said that the USC Introduction to Mindfulness course "somewhat," "much," or "very much" impacted their studying or grades (41% "much" or "very much"). It allowed them to better access academic learning tools and cope with the emotional fatigue, frustration, and anxiety that can arise with academic learning and performance.

*Resilience and confidence.* Rather than quitting when something became difficult, mindfulness gave students confidence to overcome frustrations associated with studying. "As I was getting frustrated while studying, I had this other option, which many times while studying you feel that there is no other option," Devin reflected. Meditation gave him a sense of reality and assurance that he would be alright and figure out the material in time for the test. "Many times, I would just quit, but this time even a little step away from the desk can reshape your entire perspective on the situation."

*Broadened thinking and creativity.* Reflected in Barbara Fredrickson's broaden-and-build theory, when anxiety and stress were lowered, students found they were able to better access creative and critical thinking. In the charged moments of stress and anxiety, focus narrows, and we can only see limited possibilities. Luke, a junior majoring in mechanical engineering, found that mindfulness enhanced his creativity and imagination. "The evolution of my practice has enabled me to become more aware of my body and has heightened my ability to visualize things in the abstract," he reflected. "I'm having more vivid dreams than I've ever had since childhood and my imagination and creativity are being restored to my childhood level."

*Mindful study breaks.* Students took mindfulness meditation study breaks that allowed them to refocus and better retain the material. Omar, a junior business major, found that mindfulness helped him concentrate through long periods of studying. "Midterms have been in full swing these past couple of weeks, so I have had to put in long study sessions," he remarked. He found it useful to break up long study sessions with meditation. "Doing this really allowed me to sit with myself and refocus because a lot of my studying can get frustrating and confusing. Being in this mindset of frustration for too long only hinders my progress that much more, so stepping away from it to refocus is important."

*Exam performance.* Students learned tools to deal with the pressure of high-stakes exams, which then improved their performance. Students remarked that before taking a test, they were able to take a few breaths to calm their nerves. In situations where they may have panicked, they found they now had more tools to cope with performance pressure. "I believe in more stressful situations, such as before my operations midterm, I have become much calmer and collected instead of launching into a state of panic," reflected Ava, a senior majoring in business administration in cinematic arts.

*Career-readiness.* Students remarked they were better able to meet the uncertainty that comes with graduation and looking for a job. "Even through all this uncertainty and emotional mountain, I have been able to live more in the moment," reflected Marisol, a senior economics major. "Because of my practice I have been able to go into job interviews in a calm manner knowing that I am doing my best and that is good enough. It has also made me a better listener which also helped me during my interviews."

Teaching tools to build coping skills and resiliency can help students access the academic content. Students are often expected to know how to do these things, and explicitly teaching what is implicitly expected can enhance their content knowledge and agency in the learning process.

**Reflect**

1.  What gets in the way of learning for you or your students?

2.  What would it mean for your school or organization if students learned tools to be more mindful (aware, accepting, present, curious, kind)?

3.  How might mindfulness be incorporated into your classroom or organization?

4.  Which activities discussed in this section might apply to your school or organization?

5.  Poetry Connections: What are the themes about mindfulness that are portrayed in the following poems? In what way are they similar or different?
    *   "Invitation" by Mary Oliver
    *   "Morning Meditation" by Rainer Maria Rilke

6.  Extended Study: view Andy Puddicombe's Ted Talk "All it Takes is 10 Mindful Minutes" and reflect on his message. What examples does he give to illustrate his point?

7.  Try it: Practice leading an activity from this section. Reflect on how it went and next steps.

**MODULE 1 MEDITATION: ANCHORING THROUGH THE BREATH**

As you arrive into this space,
take a breath.
Inhale.
Exhale.

Notice your breath as it enters and leaves your body.
Inhale deeply.

Notice the way the inhale changes the shape of your spine.
Exhale deeply.
The abdomen recedes back to the spine with each exhale.

Each breath is an invitation into this moment—right here, right now.
Each breath a refuge.

It's natural for the mind to wander. When it does,
notice it, and
bring the attention back to the breath,
back to this moment.
The breath as an anchor to bring you home.
Over and over again.

Let the breath move through your body.
The breath touches each cell.
Expanding to the edges, the borders, of your body—
a gentle wave washing through the whole of your body.

Now allow the attention to rest on one place of the breath,
perhaps where the breath meets the nostrils—
where it enters and leaves the body.
Notice the sensations

as the breath travels along the base of the nostrils,
the gentle expansion and release.

Each breath an invitation to come home.
To land right here, right now.

Softening into this moment.
Right here.
Right now.

**Module Reflection Form**

**Module 1: Principles of Mindfulness**

Name_____

Date/Weeks _____

1.  *Meditation Log:*

|  | Monday | Tuesday | Wednesday | Thursday | Friday | Saturday | Sunday |
|---|---|---|---|---|---|---|---|
| Initials; Minutes or Info |  |  |  |  |  |  |  |
|  | Monday | Tuesday | Wednesday | Thursday | Friday | Saturday | Sunday |
|  |  |  |  |  |  |  |  |

2.  **Meditation Reflection**. How did your practice go? What came up for you? What were the most challenging and interesting parts?

3. **Workbook Response**. Include 2-3 responses from reflection questions in Module 1. Include the question.

4. **Share**. Find an article about mindfulness and reflect on your takeaways.

5. **Questions**. (Optional)

# Bibliography

Aeidan, F., Johnson, S.K., Diamond, B.J., David, Z., & Goolkasian, P. (2010). Mindfulness meditation improves cognition: Evidence of brief mental training. *Consciousness and Cognition*, *19*(2), 597–605.

Blackburn, E.H., & Epel, E. (2017). *The telomere effect: A revolutionary approach to living younger, healthier, longer*. New York: Grand Central Publishing.

Brach, T. (2016). *True refuge: Finding peace and freedom in your own awakened heart*. New York: Bantam Press Books.

Chödrön, P. (2013a). *How to meditate*. Boulder: Sounds True.

Chödrön, P. (2013b). *Living beautifully with uncertainty and change*. Boston: Shambhala Classics.

Cohen, S., Doyle, W.J., Turner, R.B., Alper, C.M., & Skoner, D.P. (2003). Emotional style and susceptibility to the common cold. *Psychosomatic Medicine*, *65*(4), 652–657.

Colzato, L., Ozturk, A., & Hommel, B. (2012). Meditate to create: The impact of focused-attention and open-monitoring training on convergent and divergent thinking. *Frontiers in Psychology*, *3*, 116.

Condon, P., Desbordes, G., Miller, W.B., & DeSteno, D. (2013). Meditation increases compassionate responses to suffering. *Psychological Science*, *24*(10), 2125–2127.

Germer, C.K. (2009). *The mindful path to self-compassion: Freeing yourself from destructive thoughts and emotions*. New York: Guilford Press.

Goldstein, J. (2003). *Insight Meditation: The practice of freedom*. Boulder: Shambhala Classics.

Gunaratana, B. (1996). *Mindfulness in plain English*. Boston: Wisdom Publications.

International Health Conference (2002). Constitution of the World Health Organization 1946. *Bulletin of the World Health Organization*, *80*(12), 983–984.

Duckworth, A. (2016). *Grit: The power of passion and perseverance*. New York: Scribner.

Dweck, C.S. (2008). *Mindset: The new psychology of success*. New York: Ballantine Books.

Hölzel, B.K., Carmody, J., Vangel, M., Congleton, C., Yerramsetti, S.M., Gard, T., & Lazar, S.W. (2011). Mindfulness practice leads to increases in regional brain gray matter density. *Psychiatry Research: Neuroimaging*, *191*(1), 36–43.

James, W. (1890). *The principles of psychology*. New York: Henry Holt and Co.

Kabat-Zinn, J. (1990). *Full catastrophe living: Using the wisdom of your body and mind to face stress, pail, and illness*. New York: Bantam Press Dell.

Killingsworth, M.A., & Gilbert, D.T. (2010). A wandering mind is an unhappy mind. *Science*, *330*(6006), 923–932.

Kornfield, J. (1993). *A path with heart*. New York: Bantam Press Books.

Kornfield, J. (2001). *After the ecstasy, the laundry: How the heart grows wise on the spiritual path*. New York: Bantam Press Books.

Lazar, S.W., Kerr, C.E., Wasserman, R.H., Gray, J.R., Greve, D.N., Treadway, M.T., … Fischel, B. (2005). Meditation experience is associated with increased cortical thickness. *NeuroReport*, *16*(17), 1893–1897.

Lueke, A., & Gibson, B. (2015). Mindfulness meditation reduces implicit age and race bias: The role of reduced automaticity of responding. *Social Psychological and Personality Science*, *6*(3), 284–291.

Magee, R. (2019). *The inner work of racial justice: Healing ourselves and transforming our communities through mindfulness*. New York: Penguin Random House Books.

Merzenich, M. (2013). *Soft-wired: How the new science of brain plasticity can change your life*. San Francisco: Parnassus.

Moyer, C.A., Donnelly, M.P., Anderson, J.C., Valek, K.C., Huckaby, S.J., Wiederholt, D.A., … Rice, B.L. (2011). Frontal electroencephalographic asymmetry associated with positive emotion is produced by very brief meditation training. *Psychological Science, 22*(10), 1277–1297.

Nhat Hanh, T. (1992). *Peace is every step: The path of mindfulness in everyday life*. New York: Bantam Press Books.

Oliver, M. (2013). *Invitation, a thousand mornings*. New York: Penguin Books.

Puddicombe, A. (2012, November). All it takes is 10 mindful minutes. *TED: Ideas Worth Spreading*. Retrieved from https://www.ted.com/talks/andy_puddicombe_all_it_takes_is_10_mindful_minutes

Rilke, R.M., Kappus, F.X., & Maurer, K.W. (1943). *Letters to a young poet*. London: Euston Press. (Original work written ca. 1902-1908).

Shunryu, S. (2011). *Zen mind, beginners mind: Informal talks on Zen meditation and practice*. Boulder: Shambhala Publications.

Siegel, D.J. (2010). *Mindsight: The new science of personal transformation*. New York: Bantam Press Books.

Smalley, S., & Winston, D. (2010). *Fully present*. Philadelphia: Da Capo Press.

Tang, Y., Hölzel, B., & Posner, M. (2015). The neuroscience of mindfulness meditation. *Nature Reviews. Neuroscience, 16*(4), 213–225.

Thoreau, H.D. (1908). *Walden, or, life in the woods*. London: J.M. Dent. (Original work published 1854).

Yaron, L. (2015 November 11). Mindfulness in the classroom: A how-to guide. *Education Week*. Retrieved from https://www.edweek.org/tm/articles/2015/11/10/mindfulness-in-the-classroom-a-how-to-guide.html

Yaron Weston, L. (2020). Mindfulness in the classroom: Mental health and emotional resilience alongside academic studies. *Liberal Education, Association of American Colleges and Universities, 107*(3).

# Module 2    Body

*Each breath,*

*each heartbeat,*

*each cell*

*supports our being.*

*Trust the body*

*knows just what to do.*

*Let the ground*

*hold you.*

*Pause,*

*listen deeply.*

*What do you hear?*

## 2.0  Connection and Relationship to the Body

When we pause, we begin to notice what we've been carrying with us. If our bodies are at ease or in pain, if the mind is quiet or racing with thoughts, if our hearts are light or heavy. We can begin to notice it all and to trust our bodies, listen to what they are telling us, and tend to them with care.

Each second, our bodies work hard to support and balance our systems. The heart beats diligently, cells continuously repair themselves, lungs nourish the body with oxygen in each breath. And yet, so often they are ignored or treated with aggression, as we push our bodies to the maximum, without sufficient nutrients or sleep, berating them in ways we wouldn't imagine treating anyone else. We can learn to listen to our bodies, discern what signals they give us, and make choices based on the information we have. There is a knowing wisdom in nature that we are a part of. The sun rises and sets, flowers bloom, seasons change, stars sparkle, and ocean waves come to the shore. We are part of the vast ancestry and universe of life. We can learn to relax and trust in the body's wisdom that it knows just what to do.

In a meditation workshop I attended, the teacher had us ask ourselves "How are you?" And then ask it periodically again and again in meditation. This question provides the opportunity to uncover on a deeper level what might have been invisible as we plow through the days. Taking a moment to pause and check in is an invitation to deeply listen to ourselves as we would listen to a good friend.

What is the relationship we have with our bodies and how do we treat them? How do we view our age, weight, height, hair, skin color, muscular tone, or other elements of the physical self? How can we own that image and cultivate a relationship of agency, acceptance, and love? Societal ideals of body image are constructs of time, place, culture, and power. These norms can influence the relationship we have with our bodies and how we see the bodies of others. Who constructs and upholds these ideals? Who decides what and who is beautiful or handsome, or not? In what ways do race and culture intersect with beauty? What agency do we have within and outside of them? Mindful awareness can help us understand the relationships we have with our physical selves and the factors that influence them. It allows us to claim acceptance and love within our bodies and hold them with kindness.

---

Pause for a moment and take a breath

---

### Mind-Body Connection

How we care for our mental health is how we care for our physical health and is part of our integrated body system. The mind and body constantly dialogue with one another. When we feel tension in our minds, that tension and contraction can build up in the body. When we feel joy, the body may feel light and expansive.

Unprocessed emotions can manifest in different places in the physical body, including the jaw, tongue, throat, chest, or stomach. In college, my dentist noticed that I was clenching my teeth and wearing them down. I was holding stress in my jaw and throat, trying to brace, protect, or manage my fear. In yoga and meditation, I later became aware of the ways my body was holding tension. I learned to relax the physical body, which then eased my emotional tension. Correspondingly, through calming my thoughts and emotions, my body was able to relax and didn't need to hold on so tightly.

As a student athlete and sophomore business major, Emma struggled to cope with a physical injury. Through changing how she viewed it, she was able to strengthen her body and resilience to deal with physical challenges. "I am more conscientious about listening to my body/injury when running/working out and taking care of myself," she reflected. She initially felt powerless around her injury and thought there wasn't anything she was able to do about it. "It wasn't until I started exploring other ways of working out that got me out of this more negative mindset and actually made me feel stronger than before. Because of these mindfulness practices, I was able to strengthen my body and mind in ways I had not previously exercised (literally and figuratively)."

Particularly after a painful physical trauma, it is possible to experience a disconnect from the body. In his book *The Body Keeps Score*, Bessel van der Kolk writes:

> At the core of recovery is self-awareness. The most important phrases in trauma therapy are "notice that" and "what happens next?" Traumatized people live with seemingly unbearable sensations: they feel heartbroken and suffer from intolerable sensations in the pit of their stomach or tightness in their chest. Yet avoiding feeling these sensations in our bodies increases our vulnerability to being overwhelmed by them. Body awareness puts us in touch with our inner world, the landscape of our organism. Simply noticing our annoyance, nervousness, or anxiety immediately helps us shift our perspective and opens up new options other than our automatic, habitual reactions. Mindfulness puts us in touch with the transitory nature of our feelings and perceptions. When we pay focused attention to our bodily sensations, we can recognize the ebb and flow of our emotions and, with that, increase our control over them.

It can be confronting and courageous work as we explore the relationships we have with our bodies, minds, and hearts. When we make visible the unconscious and seek to understand our patterns, we can choose our responses rather than being driven by impulse or habit. Through awareness, we can practice true self-care with the energy of nurturing because it's good for us rather than the energy of not enough. It begins with examining the relationship we have with our bodies and holding them with care.

**Reflect**

1.  What is your relationship with your body like?

2.  Try it: journal on the question "How are you?"

3.  Poetry Connections: Analyze the ways the relationship between beauty, power, and society is portrayed across and within the following poems.
    *   "Yo misma fui mi ruta" ("I Was My Own Route") by Julia Burgos
    *   "If Marilyn Monroe" by Leo Romero
    *   "Phenomenal Woman" by Maya Angelou

4.    What are the societal ideals that exist for beauty and the body? Where do they come from? How are they upheld?

5.    Try it: sit for a few minutes and just notice your body. Perhaps place a hand on your heart or abdomen. Or give yourself the soothing touch of a foot or hand massage. Check in and ask how your body is doing. Reflect on what you noticed.

6.    Try it: try to increase meditation by 3–5 minutes through this module. Reflect on your experience.

## 2.1 Body Scan and Conscious Breathing Techniques

Scanning the body, bring full awareness to each area, one part at a time. You don't have to force effort into trying to relax. Gentle attention to each part can create conditions for relaxation to happen. There isn't a striving or a goal here—simply be with and hold space for the body with care. Lying down for a body scan has the advantage of allowing each muscle to passively receive, though it can also be practiced when seated or standing. Notice where your body makes contact with the surface underneath you and allow your body to be held and supported by it.

In her book *Deep Listening*, yoga teacher Jillian Pransky gives the following instruction:

> Let the earth hold you.
> No need to grip.
> No need to clench.
> No need to prop yourself up
> anywhere.
>
> Let your body land on the ground.
> Let your breath fill your body.
> The ground holds you
> so your breath can fill you.
> Feel the earth holding you.

Through body scans, we can connect with our physical selves and notice our relationship to our bodies. Do we feel connection or aversion? Are we accepting our bodies as they are or holding onto them as they were or how we want them to be? What is the quality of mind that we approach our bodies with—kind and gentle, or harsh and judgmental? If harsh tones emerge, can we hold those too with kindness?

Allow the body to be cradled by surface underneath you.
As you scan the body, bring gentle awareness to the breath,
breathing from the crown of your head,
to the base of your feet and back,
joining body with breath.
Let the breath wash through your body
just like an ocean wave coming to shore.

Give attention to each part of the body.

Bring gentle awareness to the eyes,
letting them drop back in the sockets,
inviting the muscles around the eyes and eyebrows to spread,
just like an ice cube melting.

Slowly and gently guide awareness to the temples,
cheeks,
ears,
jaw,
throat,
skull.

Down to the torso,
shoulders,
upper back,
middle back,
lower back,
chest,
abdomen,
pelvis.

The limbs,
upper arms,
lower arms,
hands and
fingers.

Upper legs,
lower legs,
feet and
toes.
Take your time,
focusing on each part.
Notice what arises as you breathe
and hold your body with care.

Variations:

• Send gratitude to each part of the body, "Thank you, eyes. Thank you, feet."
• Visualize a color or light in each body area to guide concentration as you scan the body.
• Guide attention from the outer body to the inner body of skin, muscles, bones, and nerves.
• Guide attention from the right side of the body to the left side of the body as you scan. Move from the right arm, upper arm lower arm and fingers, to the left arm.

We don't need to consciously make an effort to relax in a body scan. Simply bring awareness to each part of the body. The awareness itself can lead to more spaciousness around the area and create the conditions for relaxation to occur, though relaxation in itself is not the goal here. If you find that there are areas of tension, notice the effort of holding on. Invite space around it or envision the area spreading and softening. No need to actively force relaxation—just be with it and hold it with care.

You may find that you are dealing with pain in part of the body. Notice the sensations, and then return to a neutral place in the body that doesn't feel painful. This can be alternated, pendulating back and forth between the sensation and the neutral area. Try to soothe the pain area and hold it with care and tenderness as you might soothe a baby.

For those who have experienced trauma in the body, a body scan may be triggering, and you may find it more accessible to start with a more neutral home base, like breath or sound, or feeling your feet grounded on the floor before exploring the body. Try to be patient and hold what arises with kindness.

---

Pause for a moment and take a breath

---

### Conscious Breathing

It is estimated that humans take about 25,000 breaths each day. Breath sustains the body and is essential to our being. Each breath nourishes the body with life force. Reflective of this relationship, the Hebrew words for soul and breath are interconnected:

Soul: נשמה (neshama)
Breath: נשימה (nishema)

Current neuroscience research points to the mind-body benefits of voluntarily regulated breathing practices (VRBPs). Conscious breathing has been shown to calm the nervous system and balance body functions.

Breath becomes shallow and fast when the nervous system is activated. Deep, slow breaths relax the body by activating the calming parasympathetic nervous system and taking us out of the fight-or-flight sympathetic nervous system. Research shows a direct connection between nasal breathing and cognitive function, particularly as it relates to the hippocampus (memory) and amygdala (alarm center) brain regions. Emphasizing the exhalation has been shown to relax the vagus nerve, improve heart rate variability, and calm the nervous system. In her book *Skill in Action: Radicalizing Your Yoga Practice to Create a Just World*, Michelle Cassandra Johnson explores the breath as a resource in stabilizing the nervous system and claiming her freedom in the midst of social injustice.

When someone has experienced trauma, the breath is the most useful resource to stabilize the nervous system. The breath sends a signal that all is well; everything is okay. In a culture that would rather my black body not exist, let alone breathe, this feeling of "all is well" has been more than illusive. From the first moment I took my first breath until now, I have been on a journey to find air, to create an expansive inhale and a deepening of experience with my exhale.

The breath can transcend from the physical experience into the interconnectedness of body and breath in how we operate in the world. It can be a healing resource for coping with trauma, gaining freedom from adversity, and finding expansive acceptance. Ancient mindfulness partner practices of yoga and qigong include active, regulated breathing techniques. Though traditional mindfulness does not, practices are included here due to the vast benefits. There is no need to strive or get anywhere with the breath. Mindfulness invites us to notice the breath, where it meets the body, the way it contacts the self. Simply and gently invite the breath, letting the breath breathe you. Allow it to happen, rather than making it happen. Each breath is an opportunity to arrive in the present moment.

### Deep Breath

Take a deep breath in through the nose. Exhale let it go through the mouth. Inhale deeply, exhale deeply. Notice the sensations as the breath moves in and out through the whole of your body. Each inhalation changes the shape of your spine as the chest rises and lungs fill with air. Each exhalation a gentle release as the abdomen receeds to the spine. Deep breaths calm the nervous system and send a signal of relaxation and ease to the body.

### Nasal Breathing

Take a deep breath in through the nose. Let the breath travel along the floor of your nostrils, down your throat. Fill your lungs with air. Let the breath go, exhaling through the nose. Inhale, exhale. Notice the difference between each sensation. The nose filters and treats air and nasal breathing has been shown to lower blood pressure, regulate heart rate, and boost memory function.

### Ocean Breath

Just like a gentle ocean wave, on the inhale, allow the breath to move from the crown of your head to the soles of your feet. Exhale from the soles of your feet to the crown of your head. Let the breath wash through the whole of your body, inhaling and exhaling through the nose.

*Count Breath*

Lengthen the breath and attach a count to it. Inhale for a count of five, exhale for a count of seven. Breathe through the nose if you can. Adjust the count to what feels smooth and comfortable, not grasping for air.

*Breath Hold*

Take an easy breath in and out. Inhale deeply through the nose, hold the breath at the top for a moment, slowly exhale all the breath out through the nose. Take a few recovery breaths between each one. The hold is a gentle pause, not a grasping. If you are gasping for breath or breathing heavy afterwards, modify the length to fit the capacity of your breath.

*Alternate Nostril Breathing*

Bring your right, first two fingers in towards your palm. As one unit, place your ring and pinky finger above the left nostril (under the side bridge of the nose) so that if you press against the nose it closes the left nostril. The right thumb goes over the base above the right nostril. To open and close the nostrils, slide the fingers up and down that they maintain contact with the nose. Inhale through the right nostril as the left closes, close the right with the thumb, exhale through the left, inhale left, close left, exhale right.

*Ha Breath*

Inhale through your nose, pause slightly, exhale slowly through your mouth making a "Haaaa" sound.

*Bhramari Breath*

Take an easy breath in and out. Inhale. On the exhalation, make a low-pitched humming sound. Notice how the sound vibrates through your mouth and throat. This breath can be practiced with various hand positions over the face to direct the senses inwards. For this, place your thumbs over the base of your ears (the tragus, not inside the canal), index fingers above the eyes, middle fingers below the eyes at the sides of the nose, ring fingers above the mouth, pinky fingers below the mouth.

**Reflect**

1.  Is there a place that you typically hold tension in your body—abdomen, chest, throat, etc.? If so, what do you tend to do when it's there?

2.  When does your body feel particularly at rest and ease? What does this feel like?

3.  Try it: practice a body scan and reflect on what you noticed.

4. Try it: practice a conscious breathing technique for a few minutes and reflect on what you noticed.

5. Activity: write a letter from your body to you. What does your body want you to know? What does your body want you to do?

## 2.2  Standing, Walking, and Mindful Movement Practices

Our relationship to our bodies is reflected in how we stand, walk, and move within them. In her book *Presence: Bringing your Biggest, Boldest Self to your Challenges*, Amy Cuddy writes:

> The way you carry yourself is a source of personal power—the kind of power that is the key to presence. It's the key that allows you to unlock yourself— your abilities, your creativity, your courage, and even your generosity. It doesn't give you skills or talents you don't have; it helps you to share the ones you do have. It doesn't make you smarter or better informed; it makes you more resilient and open. It doesn't change who you are; it allows you to be who you are.

Mindfulness invites us to notice how we carry ourselves and claim agency in the integration of mind and body. It doesn't just happen while sitting with eyes closed. Standing, walking, and mindful movement can be a bridge to incorporating mindfulness in daily life as we take our practice into the world. You can do standing meditation with eyes closed or opened. If open, lower your gaze towards the floor in front of you. Walking meditation is practiced with eyes open—gaze down for inward focus or ahead to connect to the outer environment.

### *Standing Meditation*

Sense your feet on the floor.
One, then the other.
Notice the ground underneath your feet.
Allow the earth to hold you up.
Sense into all four corners of your feet.
Gently shift your weight to the right foot,
then to the left.
Shift the weight to the outsides of the feet,
then the insides,
the heels,
then the toes.
Notice the sensations on the soles of your feet.
Notice how it feels to stand in space
from the soles of your feet
to the crown of the head.
Lightly lift one leg,
and place it down.
Lift the other,
and place it down.
Come to an equilibrium between both feet.
Both grounded, held by the floor.

Begin to notice your breath
as it travels in and out through the nose.
Notice your body as it stands
bold, yet at ease.

---

Pause for a moment and take a breath

---

### Walking Meditation

Mindful walking brings awareness to how our bodies move in space. It allows us to explore the relationship we have with movement and our surroundings. I've found it to be particularly useful for times when I have a lot on my mind or when my body feels like it has too much energy at the moment to sit. Thich Nhat Hanh writes of mindful walking in his book *The Art of Power:*

> It means we learn to walk with awareness of every step we take, free of thinking and free of our projects. If you want to walk peacefully, you may take two or three steps during your in-breath. When I breathe in, I usually take two steps and say, "In, in." I say it with my feet. I don't say it aloud with my mouth. I focus my attention on the soles of my feet, with a lot of love. When I breathe out, I take two more steps and say, "Out, out." So the rhythm is "In, in, Out, Out." Touch the earth mindfully. Let your breathing be natural and coordinate your steps with your breathing. Don't stay in your head, but bring your attention down to the soles of your feet. You'll notice that your steps will be much more solid, much more stable. That stability will come into your body and your consciousness. Walk like a free person. You are no longer a slave of your projects, of your worries. Every step you take helps you reclaim your freedom.

The intentionality of mindful walking allows for stability and integration of the mind and body.

Layla, a senior majoring in law, history, and culture, noticed that mindful walking allowed her to slow down and listen to her body on her own terms. "The practice has taught me the importance of slowing down. Most of the time, I tend to ignore myself, and ignore the fact that I need to rest," she reflected. "I find myself enjoying walking meditation more than the typical ones because it gives me a sense of productivity yet also gives me a chance to wind down and check in with myself."

Like many other students on campus, Shandra, a senior in international relations, used to walk with a phone in her hand, not paying attention to her surroundings. "Usually on my way to class, I'm on my phone or having to jog to get to my classes on time," she observed. "After being introduced to mindful walking, I kept my phone in my backpack and left a little earlier, allowing me time to take in my surroundings. I enjoy mindfully walking to class because I feel less scattered when I arrive to class."

Begin by standing. Notice your feet grounded on the floor and your body in space. Choose a place of about 10–20 feet that you can walk back and forth along. This can help to relax into the rhythm of the pace without needing to think of where to go.

Standing,
notice how it feels to lift one foot off the floor,
and then then other.
When you are ready to walk,
with each step,
notice how the foot lifts off the floor,
is suspended in air,
and then returns to the ground.
Pay attention to your body
as it moves in space,
noticing your relationship to each step.
Notice the sensations of the ground underneath your feet,
your big toe, your heel.
How do they receive the earth?
Bring awareness to the movement of your body;
a foot on the ground,
then lifts,
and returns back to the earth.
Again and again.
Noticing and aware.
Nowhere to go.
Nothing to get.
No one to be.

For those who are unable to do walking meditation, explore lifting one arm, then the other, or any other sort of ongoing movement to bring an embodied mindfulness to.

**Reflect**

1. When does your body feel most at ease? How does your body feel when you are sitting, standing, walking, or moving?

2. To what extent does the way you walk or stand reflect who you are?

3. Try it: try walking or standing meditation. Reflect on what you noticed.

4.  Try it: put on some music and move your body freely. Reflect on what you noticed.

5.  Extended Study: view Amy Cuddy's Ted Talk "Your Body Language May Shape Who You Are" and reflect on her message. To what extent might this be applicable to your life?

## 2.3  Principles of Mindful Eating

Pressed for time, young adults may rush through meals, grab a bite while walking on the way to class, or skip meals altogether. When sitting down for a meal, it may be distractedly in front of the TV or phone. Mindful eating slows down the process and allows us to connect with the food we're putting in our bodies. It creates an awareness of our relationship with food and how and why we are eating. Mindfulness teacher Mitra Manesh invites students to examine *who* is doing the eating, meaning which one of our many inner selves is the one desiring the food. It might be our younger child self who was rewarded or soothed with sweets, a self who is eating to numb feelings of shame or guilt, a self who is eating to nourish the body with nutrients, or the countless inner-selves who could be fueling the desire and act of eating.

There is a freedom in doing one thing at a time and noticing that one thing with all our attention. In his book, *The Art of Power*, Thich Nhat Hanh writes about mindful eating:

> While we eat, we focus our attention on just two things: we're aware of the food and aware of our environment. We don't think of the past, we don't think of the future, and we don't think of our projects and worries. We bring all our awareness to the food and the people around us. We practice eating in such a way that joy and happiness are possible while we eat. When we pick up a piece of food, we become aware of it. We look deeply into it to see that it is a gift from the sky, the earth, and much hard work. After looking at the piece of food, we put it into our mouth and chew it carefully, mindfully. When I pick up a piece of carrot, I like to be with the carrot…I use my body and mind to pick up the piece of carrot. I look at it to recognize it as a piece of carrot. If my mind was preoccupied with other things, like my project or the past or the future, I wouldn't know that I had put a piece of carrot in my mouth…You do only one thing at a time…

In a society that glorifies multitasking and productivity, it is a luxury to bring our awareness to the one thing we are doing. The practice of mindful eating helps us notice what we are putting in our bodies and to savor the present moment. As a senior business major, Ellie learned to develop a healthier relationship with food and her body when she started pausing before eating and making more conscious food choices. "I learned to accept and embrace my food choices by learning to make more conscious decisions," she reflected. She began to ask herself how she would feel if she ate certain foods and made conscious decisions of what to eat based on that information. "I used to always beat myself up after eating unhealthy things, but by pausing and asking myself how I would feel before consuming the food, my guilt surrounding food lessened and my relationship with food and my body became much more positive."

---

Pause for a moment and take a breath

---

Mindful eating can be applied at any meal, or even just the first bite of a meal. To begin with, choose a simple fruit or vegetable, like a grape, berry, or carrot.

Take a breath and pause.
Hold it in your hand,
acknowledge how it originated,
what it took for this food to grow
from the earth,
and all the soil,
sun,
and water
that nurtured its growth.
Notice the shape, texture, temperature, and color.
Hold it up to your nose and deeply inhale the smell.
As you take a bite,
notice the texture, the taste, the temperature
and the sensations of how it feels in your mouth,
and the process of chewing.
Take your time
and savor
how it feels
to chew the food
completely,
and then swallow.
One bite at a time.

**Reflect**

1.  What is your relationship with food like?

2.  When, what, where, and how do you typically eat?

3.  What sometimes gets in the way of healthy eating?

4.  Try it: eat something simple (a grape, berry, raisin) with mindful attention and reflect on what you noticed.

## 2.4 School and Community Lens: Healthy Living

How we move, eat, and sleep fuels our bodies and can enable us to feel good, think clearly, and stay healthy. And yet, though we have all heard about the importance of eating right, exercising, and getting enough sleep, it is very easy, particularly for young adults, to skip over them. The 2015–2020 Dietary Guidelines for Americans reports:

> About half of all American adults—117 million individuals—have one or more preventable chronic diseases, many of which are related to poor quality eating patterns and physical inactivity. These include cardiovascular disease, high blood pressure, type 2 diabetes, some cancers, and poor bone health. More than two-thirds of adults and nearly one-third of children and youth are overweight or obese.

The power within this statement is the word "preventable." It's absolutely possible to develop healthy lifestyle tools and learn to treat our bodies with care so that we can live our happiest, healthiest lives. In his book *The Upward Spiral*, Alex Korb writes about the interconnection of healthy living:

> Everything is interconnected. Gratitude improves sleep. Sleep reduces pain. Reduced pain improves your mood. Improved mood reduces anxiety, which improves focus and planning. Focus and planning help with decision making. Decision making further reduces anxiety and improves enjoyment. Enjoyment gives you more to be grateful for, which keeps that loop of the upward spiral going. Enjoyment also makes it more likely you'll exercise and be social, which, in turn, will make you happier.

The interconnection of our conscious choices can lead to an upward spiral of positive benefits. Bringing awareness to how we move, eat, and sleep can have a tremendous impact on overall well-being and cognitive function.

### *Move*

Physical activity has exponential benefits for the body and mind. It has been shown to reduce the risk of disease, increase quality of life, improve sleep, maintain cognitive function, and increase happiness. Exercise leads to thousands of molecular changes that repair and support body function. The effects extend past physical. In her book *The Willpower Instinct*, Kelly McGonigal writes:

> Exercise turns out to be the closest thing to a wonder drug that self-control scientists have discovered. For starters, the willpower benefits of exercise are immediate. Fifteen minutes on a treadmill reduces cravings, as seen when researchers try to tempt dieters with chocolate and smokers with cigarettes. The long-term effects of exercise are even more impressive. It

not only relieves ordinary, everyday stress, but it's as powerful an antide-
pressant as Prozac. Working out also enhances the biology of self-control
by increasing baseline heart rate variability and training the brain. When
neuroscientists have peered inside the brains of new exercisers, they have
seen increases in both gray matter brain cells and white matter, the insula-
tion on brain cells that helps them communicate quickly and efficiently
with each other. Physical exercise—like meditation—makes your brain
bigger and faster, and the prefrontal cortex shows the largest training
effect.

Exercise provides a foundation for lifelong mind-body health. With a plethora of
workout options, it's important to find what works for you and modify to fit individual needs. Aim for a balanced approach of a combination of strength training
and cardio-respiratory fitness activities. Building muscle strength with weight-
bearing exercises (like lifting weights or doing push-ups) increases bone density,
while cardio activities (like running, biking, or hiking) helps the heart efficiently
pump blood and transport oxygen through the body. High-intensity interval training exercises, where the heart rate is elevated for a period of time, have been
found to be particularly effective. Activities like stretching or yoga can increase
flexibility and keep joints healthy and muscles supple.

### Eat

What we eat is fuel for our bodies and minds. While each person is unique in their
dietary needs, certain general principles apply when developing a healthy food plan.
Try to eat a rainbow of colors of fruits and vegetables, drink lots of water, read food
labels to limit processed and sugary foods, and aim to get an appropriate amount of
both macronutrients and micronutrients for your body. We need lots of macronutrients (protein, fats, and carbohydrates) in our diet to maintain energy for our bodies
to function and repair our body tissues. We need smaller amounts of micronutrients
(vitamins and minerals) to protect our bodies from disease, slow the aging process,
and help every system in our bodies properly function. Listen to what your body
needs and how it feels before or after eating certain foods. When in doubt, consult a
doctor or nutritionist for an individualized meal plan that fits your body.

In addition to *what* we eat, it's also important to examine *how* we eat. Rather
than eating mindlessly or unconsciously, mindful eating provides a foundation
for examining our relationship with food. Instead of skipping meals or eating in
such a rush that we don't pay attention to the food we intake, we can pause, chew
slowly, and savor each bite for the nourishment that it gives our bodies. Rather
than starving ourselves or overeating until our stomachs hurt, we can listen to
the messages our bodies give us about when, in what way, how much, and how
certain foods make our bodies feel. Over time, we can learn to slow down and
observe the sensations that arise with the food we're eating. Greater awareness
of food gives rise to the freedom to eat mindfully in full appreciation, rather than
automatically or mechanically. As for how much to eat, it can be helpful to check

in with the body periodically and rate the level of hunger/satiety, 1 being starving and 10 painfully full. Aim to eat in the 3–5 range rather than the outer edges.

As a French and political science sophomore, Legia noticed positive changes that came from mindful eating and exercise. "Due to mindful eating and working out, I have slowly been seeing an improvement in my body and in my eating habits," she observed. Over time, she began to think about how she felt before eating and paid more attention to healthy choices and portion size. "I have learned to be more aware of what I eat and where my food comes from. I have learned to listen to my body rather than my mind when it comes to eating."

## *Sleep*

Though pulling all-nighters is sometimes glorified, not getting sufficient, quality sleep takes a toll on the capacity of our minds and bodies to be able to perform at their best. When we sleep, the body repairs itself, strengthens the immune system, and enhances cognitive function. Brain scans of people who lacked sleep showed increased activity in the amygdala versus those who had gotten enough sleep, making them more likely to launch into a threat response to stressors. It also took longer for them to calm down once triggered. A study done by the Sleep and Neuroimaging Lab at Berkeley found that a good night's sleep led to being doubly effective at solving complex information patterns.

Quantity and quality of sleep can be enhanced through prioritizing this essential element of health and creating regular routines. This can be done by setting regular hours for sleeping and waking and considering adding naps to your schedule. Create a nighttime routine that allows you to unwind from the day, perhaps with journaling, meditation, restorative yoga, soothing music, a warm shower, or taking a few breaths to process and release stress. Avoid bright lights, screen time, intense workouts, heavy meals, and stimulants like alcohol and caffeine before bed. Though it may act as a sedative, alcohol disrupts the important sleep cycle of REM sleep. In the long term, healthy living principles of nutritious eating and regular exercise (though not vigorously before bedtime) can help the body sleep faster and longer.

Mindfulness can play a role in helping the body and mind to decompress before going to bed. Body scan meditation can be particularly helpful in relaxing the body before sleep. Claire, a senior majoring in business, was having trouble sleeping and started meditating before bed. "What's interesting was that I found meditation before sleep to very useful," she reflected. When she had trouble falling asleep, she discovered that meditation calmed her body and mind. "I started off with a simple inhale and exhale, then I started to feel the comfort of my bed below my crossed legs, then the air-conditioned room breezing through my skin and I just felt thankful to end my day, knowing that I will start a new one tomorrow."

---

Pause for a moment and take a breath

---

### Goal Setting Principles

If we want a different result, we have to do things differently. This takes setting an intention, making a commitment, and aligning values with thoughts, words, and actions. Kelly McGonigal writes about the power of paying attention in her book *The Willpower Instinct:*

> If there is a secret for greater self-control, the science points to one thing: the power of paying attention. It's training the mind to recognize when you're making a choice, rather than running on autopilot. It's noticing how you give yourself permission to procrastinate, or how you use good behavior to justify self-indulgence. It's realizing that the promise of reward doesn't always deliver, and that your future self is not a superhero or a stranger. It's seeing what in your world—from sales gimmicks to social proof—is shaping your behavior. It's staying put and sensing a craving when you'd rather distract yourself or give in. It's remembering what you really want, and knowing what really makes you feel better. Self-awareness is the one "self" you can always count on to help you do what is difficult, and what matters most.

Mindful self-awareness helps us notice what we crave, remember what we want, and make choices aligned with our goals. Research in goal achievement has shown that there are certain principles that can help goals stick better. They include:

1. Set realistic, specific goals that can be done in a certain amount of time. If the larger goal is "get healthier," develop specific and measurable things to reach the goal (running three days a week for 30 minutes, eating vegetables every day, etc.).
2. Clarify your intrinsic motivation. This type of internal goal is pursued because it is meaningful and inherently satisfying on a deeper level. Extrinsic goals are those that come from superficial sources or are pursued for external validation or rewards.
3. Own your goals by creating them for yourself to match your life. If possible, attach your goal to something you are already doing, like stopping at the gym after class.
4. Share the goal with others. Perhaps even choose a shared goal that you will accomplish with the support of others.
5. Doing a little bit each day is more effective than doing a lot infrequently.
6. Choose approaching, rather than avoiding goals. Ask yourself if you are doing the goal because you want to attain something or avoid something. This is the difference between someone who wants to develop healthy eating habits because they want to be healthier (approaching) or because they don't want to be overweight (avoiding). Regardless of the goal, frame it in terms of something you want to bring into your life, rather than something you don't want.
7. Celebrate the successes of the smaller goals and be flexible to adapt your goals to what is realistic to fit the life you have now and the life you want to create.

**Reflect**

1.  What does healthy living mean for you or your school or organization?

2.  What type of exercise do you do? What sometimes gets in the way of exercising?

3.  Activity: choose and register for a community fitness event or class (5k, tri-athlon, cycling race, walk, etc.). Reflect on how it went.

4.  What might it take to eat affordable, healthy, easy food in your community?

5.  Activity: share a healthy recipe. It can be a family recipe, a go-to staple, or a new one you'd like to try. Modify recipes to make them healthier (substituting brown rice or whole grains for white, replacing sugar, baking/steaming/grilling instead of frying, using "good" fats like olive oil and avocadoes, etc.). Include the ingredients, instructions, story behind the recipe, and a photo.

6.  During which hours do you typically sleep? What sometimes gets in the way of great sleep?

7. To what extent do you feel you're able to maintain habits and goals? What sometimes gets in the way? What is one habit you have that you feel good about? How did you make it stick?

8. Keep a thrive log of your exercise, nutrition and sleep for one week. Reflect on how it went.

**Thrive Log**

Date/Week:

Big goal:

Baby step sub-goal:

Reason:

Log:

|  | Monday | Tuesday | Wednesday | Thursday | Friday | Saturday | Sunday |
|---|---|---|---|---|---|---|---|
| What you did and how you felt |  |  |  |  |  |  |  |

Reflection/Observation: how did it go? How did it feel? How did you address anything that got in the way of your goal?

Next Steps: how will you continue or modify your goal? Why?

## MODULE 2 MEDITATION: BODY SCAN

*Instructions given for lying down, though can also be practiced seated or standing.*

As you settle into your space,
notice your body supported by the surface underneath it.
Let your body yield to the ground and be held by it,
heavy with the weight of gravity and cradled by the earth.

Arriving into this moment, scan your body with your breath.
From the crown of your head to the soles of your feet,
invite your body into relaxation with each inhalation,
letting the body be with each exhalation.

As you continue to breathe, gently bring awareness to your body,
with patient, kind, generous awareness.
No need to make anything happen.
Let the body be.
Invite it into this moment,
part by part.

Sense the eyes dropping back into the sockets.
Nothing needs to hold on.

Bring your attention to the muscles around the eyes,
the forehead,
the temples.
The space between the eyes and the temples.
The facial muscles spreading with each inhalation and descending with each
exhalation.
Sense the cheeks as they drop away from the nose.
Bring attention to your jaw.
Allow the tongue to fall to the back of the throat.

Each breath gently caressing the inner walls of the throat.

Sense how the breath moves through the body.
Creating space between each vertebra in the spine with each inhale.
Gentle relaxation with each exhale.
Sensing into the upper back,
the middle back,
the lower back.


The front torso open and receptive.
Sense the chest,
your heart beating, pumping blood to the whole of your being.
The abdomen,
notice the gentle rise and fall of the breath
with each inhalation and exhalation.


The arms gently at rest in shoulder sockets.
the upper arms,
the lower arms,
the hands.
Each finger—thumb, first, middle, ring, pinky.
Sensing the whole of the hands, fingers, and arms.


The legs at rest in the hip sockets.
The upper legs,
the lower legs,
the feet.
Each toe—big toe second toe, third toe, fourth toe, baby toe.
Sensing the whole of the feet, toes, and legs.


Sensing the whole of the body, receptive and spacious.
Gentle, patient, kind awareness.


Inhaling and exhaling.

**Module Reflection Form**

**Module 2: Body**

Name_____

Date/Weeks _____

1. *Meditation Log:*

|  | Monday | Tuesday | Wednesday | Thursday | Friday | Saturday | Sunday |
|---|---|---|---|---|---|---|---|
| Initials; Minutes or Info |  |  |  |  |  |  |  |
|  | Monday | Tuesday | Wednesday | Thursday | Friday | Saturday | Sunday |
|  |  |  |  |  |  |  |  |

2. *Meditation Reflection.* How did your practice go? What came up for you/ what did you notice in mindful walking and eating?

3. *Workbook Response.* Include 2–3 responses from reflection questions in Module 2. Include the question.

4.   *Mindfulness in Daily Life.* Which area of daily life would you like to apply mindfulness practice to? Areas can include: relationships and communication, mindful eating, self-care and self-compassion, mindful technology use, mindful learning, mindful decision making, or social justice.

5.   *Share.* Pick a significant quote or passage from this book to share. What does it mean to you and what implications does it have for your practice?

6.   *Questions*: (Optional)

# Bibliography

Angelou, M. (1994). *Phenomenal woman: Four poems celebrating women.* New York: Random House.

Baumeister, R., & Tierney, J. (2011). *Willpower: Rediscovering the greatest human strength.* New York: Penguin.

Buettner, D. (2012). *The blue zones: 9 lessons for living longer from the people who've lived the longest.* Washington: National Geographic.

Contrepois, K., Wu, S., Moneghetti, K.J., Hornburg, D., Ahadi, S., Tsai, M.S., … Snyder, M.P. (2020). Molecular choreography of acute exercise. *Cell, 181*(5), 1112–1130.

Cuddy, A. (2012, June). Your body language may shape who you are. *TED: Ideas Worth Spreading.* Retrieved from https://www.ted.com/talks/amy_cuddy_your_body_lang uage_may_shape_who_you_are?language=en

Cuddy, A. (2016). *Presence: Bringing your boldest self to your biggest challenges.* New York: Little, Brown and Company, Hachette Book Company.

de Burgos, J. (1997). *Song of simple truth: The complete poems of Julia de Burgos* (J. Agüeros, Trans.). Willimantic: Curbstone Press. (Original work published 1939).

De Couck, M., Caers, R., Musch, L., Fliegauf, J., Giangreco, A., & Gidron, Y. (2019). How breathing can help you make better decisions: Two studies on the effects of breathing patterns on heart rate variability and decision-making in business cases. *International Journal of Psychophysiology, 139*, 1–9.

Dietary Guidelines Advisory Committee. (2015–2020). *Dietary guidelines report.* Retrieved from https://health.gov/our-work/food-nutrition/2015-2020-dietary-guid elines

Duhigg, C. (2012). *The power of habit: Why we do what we do in life and business.* New York: Random House.

Ellenbogen, J.M., Hu, P.T., Payne, J.D., Titone, D., & Walker, M.P. (2007). Human relational memory requires time and sleep. *Proceedings of the National Academy of Sciences University of the Sunshine Coast, 104*(18), 7723–7728.

Elliot, A.J., & Church, M.A. (1997). A hierarchical model of approach and avoidance achievement motivation. *Journal of Personality and Social Psychology, 72*(1), 218–232.

Gerbarg, P. (2016, November 30). Neurobiology and neurophysiology of breath practices in psychiatric care. *Psychiatric Times, 33*, 22.

Hanh, T.N. (2008). *The art of power.* New York: Harper One.

Johnson, M.C. (2017). *Skill in action: Radicalizing your yoga practice to create a just world.* Portland: Radical Transformation Media.

Korb, A. (2015). *The upward spiral: Using neuroscience to reverse the course of depression, one small change at a time.* Oakland: New Harbinger Publications.

Krause, A.J., Simon, E.B., Mander, B.A., Greer, S.M., Saletin, J.M., Goldstein-Piekarski, A.N., & Walker, M.P. (2017). The sleep-deprived human brain. *Nature Reviews. Neuroscience, 18*(7), 404–418.

Litchfield, P.M. (2003). Brief overview of the chemistry of respiration and the breathing heart wave. *California Biofeedback, 19*(1), 1–11.

Locke, E.A., & Latham, G.P. (2002). Building a practically useful theory of goal setting and task motivation: A 35-year odyssey. *American Psychologist, 57*(9), 705–717.

McGonigal, K. (2011). *The willpower instinct.* New York: Penguin Publishing Group.

Moyer, C.A., Donnelly, M.P.W., Anderson, J.C., Valek, K.C., Huckaby, S.J., Wiederholt, D.A., … Rice, B.L. (2011). Frontal electroencephalographic asymmetry associated with positive emotion is produced by very brief meditation training. *Psychological Science, 22*(10), 1277–1279.

Pollan, Michael (2008). *In defense of food: An eater's manifesto.* New York: Penguin Press.

Pransky, J. (2017). *Deep listening.* New York: Rodale Books.

Rethorst, C.D., Wipfli, B.M., & Landers, D.M. (2009). The antidepressive effects of exercise: A meta-analysis of randomized trials. *Sports Medicine, 39*(6), 491–511.

Romero, L. (2000). If Marilyn Monroe. *The taco shop poets anthology.* Austin: Tonguefire Press.

Strachman, A., & Gable, S.L. (2006). What you want (and do not want) affects what you see (and do not see): Avoidance social goals and social events. *Personality and Social Psychology Bulletin, 32*(11), 1446–1458.

Van der Kolk, B. (2014). *The body keeps the score: Brain, mind, and body in the healing of trauma.* New York: Viking Press.

Yoo, S.S., Gujar, N., Hu, P., Jolesz, F.A., & Walker, M.P. (2007). The human emotional brain without sleep-a prefrontal amygdala disconnect. *Current Biology, 17*(20), R877–R878.

Zaccaro, A., Piarulli, A., Laurino, M., Garbella, E., Menicucci, D., Neri, B., & Gemignani, A. (2018). How breath-control can change your life: A systematic review on psycho-physiological correlates of slow breathing. *Frontiers in Human Neuroscience, 12,* 353.

Zelano, C., Jiang, H., Zhou, G., Arora, N., Schuele, S., Rosenow, J., & Gottfried, J.A. (2016). Nasal respiration entrains human limbic oscillations and modulates cognitive function. *The Journal of Neuroscience, 36*(49), 12448–12467.

# Module 3　Heart

*The heart is big enough to hold it all.*

*The joy alongside the grief,*

*and the whole spectrum of emotions*

*that make us human.*

*Courageous*

*and open-hearted*

*in the face of life*

*to feel what emerges*

*when we pay attention.*

*To listen to the heart*

*is to see*

*its vulnerability*

*and trust*

*in its resilience.*

## 3.0  Noticing and Processing Emotions

In the busyness of the day, we may not have the time or space to process emotions as they arise.

It is sometimes inconvenient and exhausting to feel. Instead, we might ignore, repress, or unconsciously react. We might want to get rid of the emotions that make us feel bad, ignore the neutral ones, and cling to the ones that feel good. While some may be more pleasant or difficult than others, emotions are not inherently positive or negative. In the full spectrum of what it means to be human, each emotion has value and can lead to deeper understanding and agency.

Tony came to understand that emotions were a vehicle for meaning and growth. "I think the coolest part of this practice is learning to just let emotions be present in the mind without trying to either hold onto them or push them away," he reflected. "Even when 'negative' emotions come up, there is a lot of value in truly understanding what that emotion feels like. I think it gives me a greater appreciation for consciousness and life. It teaches me that there can be passion and meaning in whatever emotion I feel."

It isn't about conjuring or repressing any particular emotion, but what we do with them. Aristotle writes of skillful intensity and direction of emotion in *The Doctrine of the Mean:*

> it is in emotions and actions that excess, deficiency, and the median are found. Thus we can experience fear, confidence, desire, anger, pity, and generally any kind of pleasure and pain either too much or too little, and in either case not properly. But to experience all this at the right time, toward the right objects, toward the right people, for the right reason, and in the right manner—that is the median and the best course, the course that is a mark of virtue.

While we cannot control which emotions arise, we have a choice in how we relate to them and what we do with them. Mia found that she was often swept away by her emotions. She found empowerment in being able to notice and work with them. "I actually love this idea of working with emotions. I'm someone who really feels emotions when they're happening, so much so that I often get swept up in them. As such, I honestly don't even realize what I'm feeling or how it's actually affecting me." she reflected. "However, by paying more attention to identifying my emotions, I am able to begin the process of working with them and not letting them just control me."

We may have been on the giving or receiving end of what happens when bottled up emotions explode. The natural cycle is to take in, process, digest, and then eliminate. We inhale oxygen, use what is needed, and exhale carbon dioxide. We intake food, absorb nutrients, and eliminate waste. Imagine if we didn't allow for an exhale or elimination in these circumstances. Whether breath, food, or emotions, there is a natural and necessary cycle of intake and output. When emotions are held onto or suppressed, this grasping or aversion can result in the experience being stored instead of metabolized.

It is possible to hold onto emotions for years, decades, even a lifetime. In her book *My Stroke of Insight*, Jill Bolte Taylor suggests that the lifecycle of an emotion lasts only 90 seconds. What makes it last longer is our mental replaying of the emotion or experience. It is said that there are two arrows to a difficult moment— the first is the event, and the second is our reaction to the first in a residue of replaying emotions, memories, and thoughts of what happened. It is the second arrow that can be more painful, and the one where we have an option in how we receive it. Mindfulness offers a choice and recognition that we have the capacity to let go or hold on. Christopher Germer explains this in his book *The Mindful Path to Self-Compassion* with the equation:

$$\text{Pain} \times \text{Resistance} = \text{Suffering}$$

Pain is inevitable in life, yet how much we suffer is based on resistance to what is happening. For example, say you wanted something to work out and it didn't (a grade, a relationship, a job, etc.). If you accept that it didn't work, learn the lesson, and move on, then you will suffer less than if you resisted, agonized, or wished for a different past. Through acceptance and processing, we can learn to relate to pain differently and gain more ease and freedom in our response. This is not to say that we shouldn't fight for what we want or believe in, but to acknowledge what is happening with acceptance *that* it is happening so that we can see more clearly and take wise action in the midst of it. Joseph Goldstein writes in his book *Insight Meditation*:

> So often in our society we hear and read that we need to honor our emotions, which is certainly true in the sense of recognizing, accepting, and opening to them. But that by itself is not enough. We also need to take the next step, to investigate whether a particular mind state is skillful or not. Is it bringing happiness and freedom, or is it bringing more suffering? Do we want to cultivate it, or to let it go? We always have this choice, although we often fail to exercise it. This quality of wise discrimination can empower us tremendously. We can rarely control what emotions come into our mind and heart. But once they are there, we can acquire the freedom to relate to them in different ways. If we are unaware either of what emotion is present or of whether it is wholesome or unwholesome, then we simply act out all our old patterns of conditioning. This may keep us entangled in suffering even as we are wanting happiness. When we are aware of both of these aspects, we create the possibility for wise choice and inner freedom.

Noticing emotions is the first step to discerning a skillful response. The pause between noticing and responding is the mindful awareness and freedom that comes with conscious choice. Thich Nhat Hanh writes of this in his book *The Art of Power*:

> When you notice a strong emotion arising, go back to yourself and begin the practice of mindful breathing to generate the energy of mindfulness for your

protection. Be there for your emotion and don't just let it overtake you. Don't become a victim of your emotion. It's like when you know a heavy storm is coming. You have to do everything you can to protect your house so that it won't be damaged by the wind. Strong emotions come from within, from the depths of our consciousness. The energy of mindfulness also comes from the depths of our consciousness. So you sit in a stable position, in a chair with your feet flat on the floor or cross-legged on a cushion, or you lie down, and you prepare yourself for the emotion. You begin to breathe in and out, and you focus your attention on your abdomen. Why your abdomen? When you see a tree in a storm and you focus your attention on top of the tree, you feel vulnerable. You have the impression that the tree is too fragile to withstand the storm, because the little branches and the leaves on top of the tree sway violently in the wind. You have the impression that the tree will be blown away. But if you focus your attention on the trunk of the tree, you get a different impression. You can see that the tree is solid and rooted deeply in the soil, so you know the tree will withstand the storm.

Processing emotions through skillfully working through them can deactivate emotional reactivity and create more spaciousness to digest experiences. It isn't necessarily which emotion arises, but how we work with whatever arises that allows for freedom and opening.

> Pause for a moment and take a breath

### RAIN Technique

RAIN provides a framework for working with emotions. We can notice what arises, allow it, explore how it feels in the body, and hold it with kindness and nonattachment to our identity. RAIN includes 5 steps:

1. *Recognize*: Recognize and label the emotion that is arising.
2. *Allow*: Allow and accept it, rather than pushing it away.
3. *Investigate*: Investigate how it feels in the body.
4. *Non-identify*: Try not to identify with it as part of who you are.
5. *Nurture*: Hold what arises with kindness.

#### Recognize

The first thing to do when working with emotions is to notice them. Simply recognizing the emotion is a nonreactive way of honoring what we're feeling and welcoming it as a messenger in the body. Label the emotion, whether anger or love, joy or pain, fear or trust. The subtle nuance of emotional granularity in accurately identifying an emotion can help us know what we're feeling.

When I was feeling what I thought was grief over leaving my career as a public high school English teacher, I spoke with my teacher and friend Matthew, who after a time of listening told me it didn't seem like I was feeling grief. It seemed like I was feeling guilt. He was right. With that recognition and insight to the nuance of my emotion, I was able to immediately let the feeling go. I realized that I didn't have to feel guilty and that I had rich contributions and a meaningful first phase of my career. It was time to move forward to this next and very exciting step of teaching well-being at the college level. I knew that I would find ways to contribute to K–12 education, which I have since, and that I didn't need to feel guilty. Accurate awareness is the first step in processing.

Omar also noticed that just recognizing the emotion he was experiencing gave him the choice in how to hold it. "I do feel a strong change in my general vibe and outlook after finishing a meditation session. I feel much more open to the world and interactive with others after meditating," he observed. He found that recognizing an emotion with RAIN provided more nuance to his experience. "You can feel upset, just slightly annoyed, or you can feel so upset that you are devastated. I think recognizing these nuances and depths of emotion allows me to sit with the emotion in a softer way."

### Allow

Allow the emotion without trying to resist, push, away, or make it into anything other than what it is. In her book *True Refuge*, Tara Brach depicts allowing as a form of acceptance. She writes:

> Allowing means "letting be" the thoughts, emotions, feelings, or sensations you discover. You may feel a natural sense of aversion, of wishing that unpleasant feelings would go away, but as you become more willing to be present with "what is," a different quality of attention will emerge. Allowing is intrinsic to healing, and realizing this can give rise to a conscious intention to "let be."

Notice where the emotion might be sitting in the body, whether in the abdomen, chest, throat, or head. We aren't necessarily trying to do anything with it or actively trying to let it go or release it. We're giving the emotion a little space to breathe and be.

### Investigate

Investigate the emotion. Notice the intensity, the texture, the speed, the temperature, and the flavor through curious examination. "Impatience, …this is what that feels like." Explore its qualities, whether sharp or dull, fast or slow, hot or cold, rough or smooth. Patiently sit with the emotion and listen to it: Why is it there? What is it trying to say? What does it want me to know or learn? Tara Brach goes on to write:

> Investigation means calling on your natural interest—the desire to know truth—and directing a more focused attention to your present experience. Simply pausing to ask, "What is happening inside me?" might initiate recognition, but with investigation you engage in a more active and pointed kind of inquiry. You might ask yourself: "What most wants attention?" "How am I experiencing this in my body?" or "What am I believing?" or "What does this feeling want from me?" You might contact sensations of hollowness or shakiness, and then find a sense of unworthiness and shame buried in these feelings. Unless they are brought to consciousness, these beliefs and emotions will control your experience and perpetuate your identification with a limited, deficient self.

Investigation provides the neutral space for noticing what is present. With this information, we can then determine how we view it and how we relate to it.

### Non-identify and Nurture

Release the identification and relate to it as *the* emotion, rather than *your* emotion (*the* impatience rather than *my* impatience). Instead of labeling one's self as an "impatient person," impatience is just something we may happen to be experiencing at that time. This creates a moment of separation to not take the emotion personally and not get caught in identifying with it. Emotions come and go and pass through us all the time. They are not who we are and don't define us. You are so much more than that emotion. Emotions are temporary, impermanent occurrences. This allows space to experience the feeling as one of many states of being human, without personalizing or attaching permanence to it.

Try to hold what arises with kindness and patience. As messy and uncomfortable as they may be, emotions are part of the human experience. It is a courageous act to sit with them, and we can learn to nurture ourselves in the face of our human emotions.

Lucas, a senior business major, found RAIN helped him understand how to work with his emotions. "I have been at my peak of dealing with complex emotions this past week and this module helped me understand how to approach them without dismissing them. I felt a lot more in control rather than allowing the emotions to take control of my life and what I wanted to do moving forward after thinking through them with RAIN," he reflected. Lucas was able to work through a mix of emotions including sadness, frustration, and rejection. "With this framework, I noticed the most important aspect was allowing myself to feel them rather than rejecting them and also non-identifying with them, so not associating them with myself allowed me to feel a bit better rather than falling into a hole."

## Reflect

1.  How do you relate to your emotions?

2.  Which emotions are easiest or hardest for you to attend to?

3.  What do you typically do when pleasant or difficult emotions arise?

4.   Poetry Connection: what is the attitude towards emotions that Rumi portrays in his poem "This Being Human is a Guest House?" To what extent do you agree or disagree?

5.   Try it: through this module, try increasing the time you invest in meditation by 3–5 minutes. Reflect on what you notice.

## 3.1 Causes and Conditions of Peace, Kindness, and Joy

In a Native American legend, a grandfather tells his grandchild about two wolves that fight within the heart: one vengeful and angry; the other full of kindness and love. When the grandchild asks who will win, the grandfather replies that it is the one we choose to feed. What we feed, plant, and practice is the thing that grows.

While some people may appear to be "positive" people and others "negative" people, in fact, the research on neuroplasticity and growth mindset shows that we can actually grow emotional intelligence. To place a fixed label on being a certain kind of emotional identity can be problematic when we are faced with other emotions. What do I do if I'm a happy person feeling sadness? Rather than moving through life as a positive or negative emotional type of person, aim for awareness of relating to the whole spectrum of whatever emotions arise. With this, we can learn to skillfully cultivate what is useful and work with what isn't.

Inner goodness exists within each of us. In his book *Natural Wakefulness: Discovering the Wisdom We Were Born With*, Gaylon Ferguson writes, "this path of awakening the heart is a natural process—it's going with the grain of our own basic goodness, following the movement of an instinctive desire to wake up." Through mindfulness, we can cultivate the four "abodes" of kindness, compassion, sympathetic joy, and equanimity. No matter how little or much of them we may feel in a given moment, we can explore their causes and conditions, as well as identify what might get in the way of them.

### *Equanimity*

Equanimity is an even, balanced, stability and calm in the midst of life's circumstances. It is the ability to stand in the eye of a storm and not be shaken. We may not be able to control what is happening around us, or what others are doing, but we do have control over how we choose to view it and how we respond. We can choose acceptance for what is happening and release the struggle to see things differently than what they are.

Acceptance does not mean resignation, passivity, or indifference. On the contrary, equanimity is a courageous practice of clear seeing and wise discernment. When we can see more clearly and untangle our own identification and egos, we can discern a wise path of action. Tara Brach writes of this in her book *Radical Acceptance*:

> Clearly recognizing what is happening inside us, and regarding what we see with an open, kind, and loving heart, is what I call Radical Acceptance. If we are holding back from any part of our experience, if our heart shuts out any part of who we are and what we feel, we are fueling the fears and feelings of separation that sustain the trance of unworthiness. Radical Acceptance directly dismantles the very foundations of this trance.

When we can clearly see what is happening, then we can take skillful action to choose our response. Clear responses can be clouded by resentment, aversion to what is happening, or attachment to how we think things should be rather than how they are. Equanimity is an acceptance so that we can have a choice in how we respond.

Just as the breath, body, or sound can be a directed anchor in practice, we can also use a repeated word or phrase to ground our attention.

"May I accept that things as they are."
"It is what it is; it was what it was."
"May my heart know peace."
"May my heart continue to open."

Choose one or more of the phrases to repeat in meditation—or create a phrase that resonates for you. Notice your reaction and response to it. We are not trying to conjure anything, just an awareness for what arises and a measure of spaciousness as we sit with it. Though phrases are repeated, try to say each one with individual attention and meaning as if for the first and last time.

### Kindness

The Pali word *metta* is often translated as loving kindness, benevolence, or friendliness. In his book *Mindfulness*, Joseph Goldstein writes of metta as the:

> generosity of the heart that simply wishes all beings to be well and happy. Metta helps prevent the arising of aversion because it focuses on the good in people rather than their faults. Sometimes people think that if we have too much loving kindness, always focusing on the good in others, it will make us stupid in some way, that we'll no longer see the truth of what is going on or be able to take appropriate action. But it is precisely the mind not clouded by anger or hatred that allows us to see situations clearly and to chart the right course of action, even in difficult situations. It is important to realize that all aversion does not fall away with our first loving wish...As loving kindness grows stronger, both for ourselves and others, we feel more tolerance, are a little less judgmental, and slowly and gradually start to live in a growing field of benevolence and goodwill. Here is where metta as a dissolver of aversion also becomes the ground for wisdom. The more loving and patient we are with difficulties and disturbances, the less lost we are in our reactivity. Our choices and actions become wise, which in turn leads to more happiness, more metta, and greater freedom.

Kindness opens the heart and allows for clear seeing and freedom. We can wish ourselves well and send that kindness to others. Some may find that it is easier to send it to others than themselves. Some may find it is easier to send it inwards than outwards. Whatever arises, try to hold it with curiosity and kindness. Metta practice traditionally takes the form of phrases of well wishes.

"May I/you be happy."
"May I/you be healthy."
"May I/you be safe and protected."
"May I/you live with peace and ease."

You can also develop your own phrases that resonate for you. Begin this practice with sending kindness to a person or a pet you find easy to like. Then, try sending kindness to yourself (perhaps from them to you). If you notice any resistance, just simply recognize the emotion, send yourself some kindness, and remind yourself that you are indeed worthy of it. You can send it to a mentor, teacher, or benefactor. And then even to a neutral person. If you feel ready, send it to a difficult person (perhaps just lightly/moderately difficult to start). Lastly, include all beings.

Matthew Brensilver instructs that like a magnet, metta practice will bring to the surface all the things that aren't it that we've been holding onto in our hearts. This gives us information about what gets in the way of opening our hearts. Whatever arises, we can hold space with gentleness and patience in the process of freeing the heart.

### Compassion

Compassion meets difficulties with kindness. Compassion is not weakness or pity. It is not an overwhelming tide of sorrow. With compassion, we actively bear witness to pain and hold kind space around suffering. In Sharon Salzberg's book *Lovingkindness: The Revolutionary Art of Happiness,* she writes:

> Sometimes we think that to develop an open heart, to be truly loving and compassionate, means that we need to be passive, to allow others to abuse us, to smile and let anyone do what they want with us. Yet this is not what is meant by compassion. Quite the contrary. Compassion is not at all weak. It is the strength that arises out of seeing the true nature of suffering in the world. Compassion allows us to bear witness to that suffering, whether it is in ourselves or others, without fear; it allows us to name injustice without hesitation, and to act strongly, with all the skill at our disposal.

To be human is to suffer. No one is exempt. How do we witness and hold this pain? How do we turn towards a difficult moment and meet it with kindness? In 2020, as cities across America went from isolation of the pandemic to protesting racial injustice, what did it mean to bear witness to the suffering? What did it mean to individually and collectively hold space for the grief, frustration, fear, anger, and resistance that arose? And, how do we channel that energy into wise words and actions?

In her book *The Inner Work of Racial Justice: Healing Ourselves and Transforming our Communities Through Mindfulness,* Rhonda Magee defines justice as "love in action for the alleviation of suffering." Justice is thus an active response prompted by compassion in seeing the suffering of others. She writes:

> Racial justice, like compassion, is just one form of an ethically grounded, mindful response to the suffering in our lives. Moreover, mindful racial justice seeks to alleviate not merely isolated incidents of racial suffering, but all suffering caused by racism—including suffering that is very hard to see... Racial justice cannot exist apart from the effort to alleviate the socially constructed, unevenly distributed suffering of all marginalized people, or what I would call "social justice." And social justice cannot exist apart from racial justice.

How do we see and hold individual and collective suffering? Where equanimity asks us to clearly see and accept the truth of what is happening, compassion meets the suffering with kindness. They together ask what the kind and wise response is. How do we meet such moments of difficulty, and what do we do next?

*Self-Compassion*

We are who we are—not in spite of, but because of the challenges we have faced. We can learn to meet our difficulties with kindness, to not to be so hard on ourselves, and that we are human and don't need to be perfect. Through self-compassion practices, Jackson found that he could treat himself with the kindness and acceptance that he shows to others. "I have learned how to treat myself like how I treat my friends," he reflected. "Instead of being too self-critical to myself, I learned that I cannot be perfect in everything I do, and it's okay," he discovered. "With such a mindset, I actually find myself doing better at things because I am not worried about doing everything in a 'perfect' form."

Self-compassion includes three components:

1. *Mindfulness*: Notice the moment of challenge or difficulty. Hold it with awareness and nonjudgmental acceptance.
2. *Kindness*: When difficulties arise, we can either meet them with harshness and be hard on ourselves, or we can meet the moment with kindness. Just as we might comfort a friend, we can soothe ourselves, place our hands on our hearts, and say, "I've got you." "I'm here for you." "Everything will be ok."
3. *Shared humanity*: We each have our own battles, we all face challenges, and we all make mistakes. We can recognize that the difficulties we face are both uniquely personal and also have been felt, and are being felt, by so many others. We can send kindness to us and them. For all the students who have been anxious before an exam, or a presentation, or a date, can we hold the shared experience and emotion with kindness for us all?

In her book *Self-Compassion: The Proven Power of Being Kind to Yourself*, Kristin Neff, self-compassion researcher, offers the following phrases for cultivating self-compassion in practice:

"This is a moment of suffering."
"Suffering is a part of life."
"May I be kind to myself in this moment."
"May I accept this moment exactly as it is."
"May I accept myself in this moment exactly as I am."
"May I give myself all the compassion and courageous action I need."

Through self-compassion, we can realize that mistakes happen to everyone, and we can love ourselves no matter what. In his book *The Mindful Path to Self-Compassion*, Christopher Germer offers the following phrases:

"May I love myself just as I am."
"May I love and be loved."
"May I care for myself with ease."
"May I find peace in this uncertain world."
"May I have happiness and the causes of happiness."
"May my happiness continue to grow."

Luke noticed that he suppressed his emotions so as not to appear sensitive. Through self-compassion practice, he grew to have more love and appreciation for himself and others. "I noticed I was more sensitive and emotional than I wanted to admit to myself at the time, and over time I think I have toughened up and have tried to suppress my own emotions by telling myself that things don't matter much and simply avoiding them," he reflected. Luke began repeating a phrase to himself in meditation, "May I be loved," and noticed that it initially felt unsettling to him. "This simple phrase, while a positive affirmation of value and worth, was also a reminder that often times I don't feel loved or appreciated by the people around me. However, with a focus on mindfulness applied to self-compassion and affirming self-worth I have found a greater appreciation for the interactions I am able to share with those around me on a daily basis."

## *Joy*

Joy does not exist outside of ourselves. It isn't in our material possessions or based on our external circumstances of which school, job, grade, relationship, or items we have. We may think that when certain external conditions are met, or when life is calmer, then we can feel joy. But that kind of satisfaction fades. We may have experienced this when we very much wanted something, but a while after getting it, happiness diminished over time and we eventually went back to our baseline happiness before we had it. This is known as hedonic adaptation. To keep up with this type of satisfaction, we would have to run on a hedonic treadmill, continually getting things, more things, better things, bigger things to try to satisfy that craving, but ultimately not finding sustainable satisfaction from them. Joy is our birthright and is available in this very moment of present awareness. Can we notice the bright blue sky, the sun on our skin, the smell of a rose, the warm hug of a friend? Even in the midst of difficulty, can we pause to notice the beauty that exists and welcome the invitation of joy?

Diego, a junior majoring in political science experienced low confidence and unhappiness prior to mindfulness. Through shifting his perspective, he increased his capacity for joy. "My practice has made me such a happier person," he noticed. The prior semester, he experienced what he felt was one of his lowest points in life in terms of joy, security, and self-confidence. "One of my biggest strengths that I have rediscovered through this class is a revamped sense of happiness, gratitude, and optimism."

Though it may seem common practice to think that after we achieve certain goals that we'll be happy, happiness itself can have a role in our success. In their research, psychologists Sonja Lyubomirsky, Laura King, and Ed Diener conclude that those who feel happy tend to be more successful in various areas of life, including relationships, work, and health. A review of research found that genetic predisposition accounts for about half of our happiness level. Life circumstances, activities, and perspective accounts for the other half. While we cannot change our genetics, we can play an active role in cultivating happiness through what we do and how we view events. This is not to discount the very real chemical imbalances of depression or mental illness that make it seem impossible to feel joy. It doesn't downplay the incredible suffering that occurs in life on an individual and systemic level. Rather, it is to say that in spite of, and perhaps because of the pain, we can learn to train ourselves to see and receive joy exactly as it is.

Gratitude helps us savor joy. Instead of looking at what we don't have or comparing ourselves to others, we can focus on what we do have in this moment. We can start to retrain ourselves to view experiences with abundance, rather than scarcity. We don't need to grasp it or fear that it will end. When we experience joy, we can learn to savor it for the time it is there. The transitory nature of all things makes savoring that much more important knowing they won't last forever. Psychologists Fred B. Bryant and Joseph Veroff describe savoring as the "awareness of pleasure and of the deliberate conscious attention to the experience of pleasure." We can learn to savor moments of joy through receiving it. They provide five techniques for savoring:

1. *Share with others*: tell others how much you value and enjoy the moment.
2. *Build memories*: take mental photographs of joyful moments that you can return to and reminisce about later with others.
3. *Congratulate yourself*: remind yourself how long you've waited and worked for this to happen.
4. *Sharpen perceptions*: focus on sensory elements of the experience. What do you see, hear, smell, taste, and touch?
5. *Absorb the moment*: get immersed in the moment and try to be in the flow of the moment without thinking.

Generosity exhibits this openhearted quality of joy. It is when we can live from a place of abundance and non-grasping that we can truly give. We can be generous with our time, our listening, our patience, our forgiveness, and our love—for others and ourselves. Can we deeply listen to what we are feeling and have generous patience to hold ourselves with kindness and love?

## Sympathetic Joy

Just as we can learn to see, savor, and cultivate our own joy, so too can we be aware of how we respond to the joy of others. When others share their joy with us, what does it bring up for us? Can we hold their joy with happiness? The more we learn about how to hold our own joy and appreciate the preciousness of our own moments, so too can we do so for others. Research by psychologists Shelly Gable, Gian Gonzaga, and Amy Strachman found that how good news is celebrated can impact relationships. They categorized responses into four types:

1. *Active constructive*: expresses enthusiasm and interest, wants to know more.
2. *Passive constructive*: validates response with a "good job" type of comment. No enthusiasm or follow-up questions.
3. *Active destructive*: expresses concern about it.
4. *Passive destructive*: ignores the news.

The study found that active constructive responses to good news increased connection in relationships. The next time someone shares good news with you, express enthusiasm and ask questions to share in their good fortune and grow the relationship.

If someone shares news that they received an A or internship, when you really wanted one but didn't receive one, it may be difficult to hear. Try to hold what arises with self-compassion and receive it with an abundance mindset, remembering that there are plenty of good grades and internships out there. We can feel joy in the happiness of our good friends and those we care for, and over time, we can learn to also do this for those we know less well or even not at all. Their joy becomes our joy and thus magnifies and ripples outward.

---

Pause for a moment and take a breath

---

## Obstacles to Joy

Joy can be a surprisingly complex emotion. We may be so fixated on trying to hang onto the joy we have that we may hold it too tightly or forget to savor it for the time we have it. We may not believe ourselves to be worthy of the joy, or perhaps we may be waiting for the other shoe to drop. Looking at what gets in the way of it can help us learn to fully receive it.

*Impermanence and Foreboding Joy*

The fear of loss is sometimes so painful that it constricts the breath of joy. We love what we have, and we may grasp, hold, and worry about losing it so much that we choke it to death. In her book *Daring Greatly*, Brené Brown discusses "foreboding joy" when we fear something happening that might end our joy. Uncertainty and change are hard to accept when we cling to keep what we have. And yet, the only way to really enjoy is to realize that everything changes and all we have for certain is the present. When we appreciate this very moment, we realize that we don't have to hold joy too tightly and can relax into it.

*Unworthiness*

Sometimes we might not feel worthy of joy. What have we done to deserve all this happiness? The truth is that we don't need to do anything to be deserving—were born worthy. And still, it may be hard to feel joy when we notice all the suffering in the world or in the lives of people around us. Who are we to feel joy when there are so many people feeling pain? Do we have a right to joy when others are just struggling to survive? In truth, our hearts are big enough to hold it all. We can hold space for the suffering of others with compassion in our hearts, and at the same time still open to all the happiness that life offers. Our suffering will not aid in others feeling better, but our joy will increase the measure of happiness in the world.

As a senior, Soo noticed that her happiness was attached to guilt. This awareness enabled her to appreciate joyful moments by learning to work with the feelings underlying it. "Often in the past, I would feel quite guilty when I felt happy. I would question, should I be feeling this way? Should I try to take care of the next thing coming up?" Soo equated feelings of happiness with neglecting priorities like homework, studying, or applications. "I have noticed that I have confused or equated worrying with being productive and taking actions that would complete what has to be done," she observed. Worrying and feeling guilty gave Soo a false sense of peace and accomplishment that she was doing something. Though guilt was initially motivating to help her get to the next task, it was unsustainable and over time she found that not appreciating happy moments led to her feeling stressed or burned out. "So now, whenever I feel happy, I appreciate the feeling. If the feelings of guilt start to emerge, I would tell myself that feeling guilty is only giving me a peace of mind and that I am not actually doing anything that would help. I am only reducing the enjoyment of my downtime and enhancing my stress, potentially harming how productive I could be in the long run."

*Not Enough*

In our culture of more, do, and not enough, it's easy to get caught up in how to get even more joy. Sometimes we're so busy planning for more joy that we bypass the very joy we're in. One New Year's Day, on a beautiful hike in the midst of majestic mountains, I found myself thinking about how I could go for more hikes and planning the next one in my mind. Though I was in the midst of the very joy I wanted, I was thinking ahead to how I could get more of the joy I was experiencing at that moment. Planning for more joy was not the same as enjoying the moment of joy. Joy isn't something that we can horde or accumulate more of and store for the future. Joy increases the more we learn to savor our moments with generosity.

**Reflect**

1.  How do you relate to pleasant emotions? What do you do when you feel joy?

2.  What brings you joy? What gets in the way of joy for you?

3.  Poetry Connection: what is the philosophy towards joy portrayed in Mary Oliver's poem "Don't Hesitate"? To what extent do you agree or disagree?

4. Activity: list three things you're grateful for every day for a week.

|  | Monday | Tuesday | Wednesday | Thursday | Friday | Saturday | Sunday |
|---|---|---|---|---|---|---|---|
| Grateful for |  |  |  |  |  |  |  |

5. Activity: write a gratitude letter or send a gratitude text to someone you appreciate. Include a specific thing you are grateful for and what it means to you.

6. Try it: pick a practice to cultivate kindness, self-compassion, equanimity, or joy and include it in your daily practice for a week. You may need to try it a few times before you feel comfortable with it. Reflect on what you noticed.

## 3.2  Working with Difficult Emotions

In 1968, Fred Rogers debuted his song, "What do you do with the mad that you feel?" on his iconic children's television show *Mr. Rogers' Neighborhood*. This question is central to our emotional freedom. When a difficult emotion arises, we may feel consumed by it, or oppositely, we may want to ignore it or push it away. We might protect ourselves and develop armor to blunt things that we are not willing or able to feel. This can take the form of an outside distraction like shopping, video games, emotional eating, substance use, or keeping busy to avoid the feeling. While it may seem helpful to redirect attention away from a charged emotion initially, doing so in the long term will only serve as a band-aid of the symptom. Armor after armor is piled on over a lifetime of doing this, as protective mechanisms begin to restrict the freedom to live spaciously in the world. This creates a density, a weight, a hardening, and blocks the natural flow of emotion and energy.

Though we may not be able to control whether or not challenging situations or emotions arise, we can choose our relationship to them and what we do with them. How we notice, hold, and interact with the human experience of emotions can make way for transformation and growth. We don't need to suppress difficult emotions, and we also don't need to let them drive our lives. We can recognize they're there and make a conscious choice about how to hold the experience and what to do next.

In challenging times, it's not what happens that makes the most difference in our outcomes— it's how we deal with what happens and what we believe about it. Holocaust survivor and psychologist Viktor Frankl is attributed with the quote, "Between stimulus and response there is a space. In that space is our power to choose our response. In our response lies our growth and our freedom." Power and freedom come from learning to respond, rather than react. Emotions then don't just passively happen to us; they alchemize with our awareness to transform into wisdom.

In trying to ease her pain, Soo used to suppress unpleasant emotions. She found that rather than going away, they magnified. It was when she learned to allow her emotions that she was able to find clarity around them. "In the past, when I experienced unpleasant emotions that I didn't want to experience, such as frustration, anger, or sadness, I would try to suppress the emotions," she reflected. She found that she tried to bypass difficult emotions and take steps to resolve situations without acknowledging the feelings underlying them. "I wanted to take steps to resolving the conflict causing these emotions so I would try to suppress the emotions so that I can think about these steps. However, I soon noticed that suppression of those emotions would amplify them," she discovered. "Now, I have found that when I allow myself to feel these emotions, it gets the feeling out of myself and I can approach a problem with a clearer mind."

Through mindfulness, we can notice and work with emotions to create more spaciousness around them. Letting go is not an active goal or something to strive for; it's more of a letting be of what arises. Notice sensations with RAIN as your body processes the experience. Recognize the emotion arising, allow it, investigate with curiosity how the emotion feels in the body, and hold it with kindness without identifying with it as part of who you are. Take a moment to pause, notice, observe how it feels in the body, and then act (or not act) from this place.

### GOBB Technique

When feelings of overwhelm arise, take a moment to get grounded. Orient yourself in the space you are in and activate your senses. Tune in to your body and invite the breath into any areas of constriction. This is what I call the *GOBB Technique.*

- *Ground*: get grounded as you notice the surface of the ground underneath you. Sense your feet secure on the floor below.
- *Orient*: orient yourself to the space around you. Activate your senses to curiously notice what you see, hear, or smell. Note specific objects (red shoes, square tile, blue sky, etc.).
- *Body*: check in with your body to sense how it feels. Where does it feel free or constricted? Scan your body and notice any sensations.
- *Breath*: consciously tune into your breath and take 5–10 deep, slow breaths in and out through the nose.

It is important to note that sometimes an emotion might be too raw, or we may not be ready to sit with a particular emotion, especially one that is associated with trauma. Go gently so as to avoid flooding or overwhelming the body, mind, and heart with more than it can handle at the time. Take a walk or journal to switch gears until you're ready to sit. Work with a trained professional as needed.

To be human is to experience hurt. In Margery Williams Bianco's book *The Velveteen Rabbit*, the Skin Horse tells the Rabbit that being real sometimes hurts. Real is something we become over time through our experiences. We can embrace the whole spectrum of our human existence, including the hurts. Though it would be much easier if we could learn all the life lessons from the lovely moments, how we learn to endure difficulties, alongside the joy, contributes to becoming who we are.

---

Pause for a moment and take a breath

---

### Stress

With a growth mindset, we can explore our relationship to stress and learn to recognize, understand, and work with it. In her book *The Upside of Stress,* Kelly McGonigal concludes that rather than avoiding stress, we should examine how we relate to it and the meaning we can extract from it. She writes:

We cannot control the stress in our lives, but we can choose our relationship to it…Embracing stress is an act of bravery, one that requires choosing meaning over avoiding discomfort…It's not about being untouched by adversity or unruffled by difficulties. It's about allowing stress to awaken in you these core human strengths of courage, connection, and growth…People who are good at stress allow themselves to be changed by the experience of stress. They maintain a basic sense of trust in themselves and a connection to something bigger than themselves. They also find ways to make meaning out of suffering. To be good at stress is not to avoid stress, but to play an active role in how stress transforms you.

Stress isn't something that happens to us, but rather is something that we can actively reframe to find freedom in our actions within it. This isn't to discount the very real stress that is experienced, but rather to gain agency in exploring how we interact with it. Strong emotions may emerge, especially before a test, interview, or performance. In stressful situations, McGonigal advises to:

- Identify what it is you care about in the situation. Stress is a response that arises when what we care about its at stake. By identifying what it is we care about, we can better understand the motivation behind emotions and reactions.
- Recognize that stress is your body's way of mobilizing resources to help you perform, as physiological and psychological resources are directed towards helping us make it through the challenge.
- Visualize turning nerves into feelings of excitement. Say "I'm so excited," rather than "I'm so nervous." Research shows that this method of anxious reappraisal can reframe the situation and our feelings associated with it.
- Trust that you have what it takes to do your best. You do.

Additional Techniques

- Pause and take a few slow, deep breaths. Use the STOP technique (Stop, Take a breath, Observe, Proceed).
- Notice and observe any sensations, thoughts, or emotions that are present.
- If big emotions are present, use the RAIN technique (Recognize, Allow, Investigate, Non-identify, Nurture).
- Release emphasis on the result and focus on effort and skill.
- Stand tall and take a power stance (hands on hips or overhead) to send biofeedback to your body that you can do it.
- Recognize the shared humanity of others who have been or are experiencing similar situations or emotions.
- Send a little kindness and compassion to yourself and others.
- Take a walk, exercise, dance, or move your body to discharge stored energy.

After a stressful situation, we may obsess over how we did. This is an opportunity to practice equanimity, perhaps with phrases like, "It is what it is. It was what it was." At the end of the day, we do the best we can, with who we are, at that point in time, with the circumstances we have. And that's all that we can do.

(Corresponding Section: 4.4 Stress Resilience)

*Fear*

Moreso than suppressing fear, we can seek to understand it and the relationship we have with it. When fear arises, notice it and try to discern where it's coming from. Fear is a signal of danger. It can be a real danger of the threat of life at stake, or it can be a fear rooted in something else. Fear often accompanies a worry or anxiety that something may happen in the future. Notice the felt sensations that arise with it in the body and sit with it, alongside it and listen to what it has to say. Try to meet it with a compassionate response, perhaps reflecting on the following questions:

- What is at stake? What is it that I fear?
- Where is the fear coming from?
- What message is the fear communicating?
- What is the function of fear in my life? What power does it have?
- What is my relationship to fear?
- Is it true? Is it useful? Who would I be without it? How would that change my life?

(Corresponding Section: 4.1 Uncertainty and Anxiety)

*Anger*

What we project outward is also what we consume. When we direct anger towards another, we likewise experience it ourselves. As our muscles tense and heart races, our whole bodies participate in the physiological response. It may feel powerful to direct it outward, and we may think that expressing it will help to get it out of us. However, it is important to remember here that the thing we practice is the thing that grows. In feeding the root of anger, we are planting those seeds. The power lies in the freedom of choosing a conscious response. This does not mean that we suppress our anger. Anger gives us information and energy that can be a powerful catalyst for change. We can recognize it and know that we are not our anger. It is something we are experiencing that we can learn to channel into action and transformation.

It can be helpful to examine what is underlying anger. Grief may be present in what we lost, or fear of what might happen, or feelings of injustice. Anger may accompany self-righteousness—I can't believe they did that! How could they? How could they do that to me? Who do they think they are? It threatens our identity of how we think things should be, and how we think others should operate. When faced with the anger of another, we can recognize their suffering and meet it with compassion by listening to what is underlying their anger. When we are angry with ourselves, we can also hold that too with kindness? Can we channel the energy of anger into wise action?

We can recognize the emotion, and at the same time not be hooked by it or controlled by it. We can also explore what it is that we haven't accepted in the situation. Acceptance doesn't mean that we condone what happened, but that we accept *that* it happened and from there choose a conscious response.

## Forgiveness

Forgiveness does not mean approving of behavior or allowing someone hurtful back into our lives. It means that we no longer give that person or event power over us when we accept what happened and release the resentment around it. Holding onto resentment only hurts ourselves. Nelson Mandela is attributed with saying that "resentment is like drinking poison and then hoping it will kill your enemies." Forgiveness isn't as much about the other person, as much as it is an empowering gift of freedom that we give to ourselves when we decide not to let them hurt us anymore. In his book *No Time Like the Present*, Jack Kornfield describes the interconnectedness of forgiveness and freedom through honoring our experience and holding it with kindness. He writes:

> To forgive and be free, you must honor your measure of grief, betrayal, the whole difficult story, and hold it with all the compassion you can. Remember that you are bigger than anything that happens to you. Then you can turn your heart towards forgiveness.

We can hold our anger, grief, and pain with kindness and care and begin the path of healing. In forgiveness meditation, we can start with the ways we may have harmed others or made mistakes. We can acknowledge that we are learners in this world, recognize how we may have caused suffering, and ask for forgiveness. We can then offer forgiveness phrases to others. When we forgive ourselves, it creates safety in our relationships that we and others can make mistakes and still be accepted. Phrases can include:

"May I forgive myself/you for making mistakes."
"May I accept that I am/you are a learner still learning life's lessons."
"May I forgive myself/you for the harm I/you have done, knowingly or unknowingly."
"And if I cannot forgive myself/you now, may I do so sometime in the future."

We can acknowledge the pain we have been carrying and extend forgiveness. Whatever arises, try to hold it with kindness.

## Sadness

Like a wet blanket, sadness can cover us and immerse us within it. Meet it with the tenderness of self-compassion and hold what arises with kindness. Recognize that sadness is there, and that it's part of our shared human condition. Remember that emotions and circumstances are temporary and will pass. Perhaps sit alongside

the sadness, place a hand on your heart, and send phrases of self-compassion—
"I'm here for you. I've got you. This is a moment of suffering. May I be kind
to myself within it." Take deep breaths in and out through the nose. Feeling the
feelings is a courageous practice. We can feel them without suppressing them or
being swallowed by them. We can remember that we are more than one feeling,
one experience, or one moment. Reach out to a friend or take a walk to shift perspective. Prolonged, deep sadness may indicate a deeper challenge. Work with a
trained professional, and seek help when needed.

**Reflect**

1.  How do you currently deal with difficult emotions?

2.  Which difficult emotions are easiest or hardest for you to cope with? Why?

3.  If a friend or child were going through difficult emotions, what would you say to them?

4.  Activity: write a forgiveness letter to yourself or someone you want to send forgiveness to. Include what it is you are forgiving and why. You can choose to give it to them or not.

5.  What do you do before a test or challenge to deal with emotions that may arise?

6.  Try it: envision yourself before a test or challenge. What would you do or tell yourself?

7.  Try it: use the RAIN technique (Recognize, Allow, Investigate, Non-identify, Nurture) or GOBB technique (Ground, Orient, Body, Breath) to work with an emotion. Reflect on what you noticed.

## 3.3  Mental Health and Mindfulness

Just as we can cultivate physical health through effort and practice, we can also enhance mental health and well-being. Mental health is an essential component of overall health. Just as working out to increase physical health is seen as a positive investment, there should be no shame or stigma in working to strengthen mental health.

Jamar, a sophomore business major, shifted how he viewed mental health as he became more mindful. "Prior to taking this course, I simply would have defined mental health as how happy someone felt on average. However, I now know that mental health is so much more than that," he observed. He found that mental health involves all of one's social, emotional, and psychological thoughts and behaviors. "Mental health is something that everyone including myself should watch out for. I care for my mental health through meditation and communication. Meditation enables me to take a few moments each day to gain clarity. I also am working on communicating my thoughts and feelings as opposed to oppressing them."

The National Alliance for Mental Illness (NAMI) reports that 75% of all mental health conditions begin before the age of 24. Young adulthood is a foundational time to build mental health tools.

When we sit in silence with our experiences, it can be overwhelming at times. In this case, it may be helpful to pause and try one of the following trauma-sensitive practices:

1.  Pendulate between the emotion or thought, and then back to a neutral place. It may be too much to stay with an intense thought or emotion, and if so, alternate between it and a neutral home base, like the body, breath, or sound.
2.  Bring to mind an image of someone supportive to visualize next to you as you practice. It can be a kind person in your life or a person from history or religion. You can also visualize being in a safe, calming place in nature like an ocean, lake, forest, mountain, or another place you feel secure in. Imagine the sights, smells, a gentle breeze, and the sun on your skin.
3.  Use your senses to ground you with the GOBB technique. Ground yourself by bringing your attention to the soles of your feet. Orient yourself to the space you're in through your senses—what do you see, hear, feel, smell, or taste? Perhaps count colors or shapes of objects around you. Tune into your breath and body.
4.  Use the RAIN technique to work through difficult emotions that arise. Recognize or label the emotion, allow it without resisting or pushing away, investigate how it feels in your body and where it might be sitting, try not to take it so personally (*the* emotion, rather than *my* emotion), and hold what arises with kindness.
5.  Try to release judgment around the situation. Rather than judging yourself for feeling a certain way or trying to suppress the emotion, approach it with kind curiosity, knowing that each moment or state is temporary, and we do the best we can.

6. Discern what you have control of in the situation. In contrast to helplessness or imagining that a feeling or experience will impact every area of your life, try to find something you can take active control of, even if it might be your perspective, to find meaning in the experience. Try not to universalize or personalize the feeling with shame or blame. This is the difference between I made a mistake or *did* something bad versus I *am* a bad person.
7. Practice self-compassion. When faced with a difficult emotion, thought, or situation, hold it with kindness and recognize the shared humanity of all the other people who may be struggling with a similar experience.
8. Mix it up. If seated meditation is difficult, try standing, walking, or mindful movement. Switch up your surroundings and get some sunshine or go to a place you feel good about being in.
9. Take time to care for you. Spend time in nature, go for a walk, exercise, eat a nourishing meal, get a good night's sleep, or connect with a friend.
10. Seek help when needed. Know you are not alone and that there are people to support you. Reach out a therapist or trusted teacher or friend when needed. Remember that everyone is fighting their own battles, and we are all in it together.

Noah, a senior majoring in economics, found that mindfulness helped him build mental health and increase his capacity to work through challenges with kindness. He reflected, "I feel more equipped to handle times of bad thoughts or anxiety, and welcome and work through them with kindness." Likewise, Shandra, found that recognizing her emotions and experiences, rather than suppressing them, helped her build mental health resilience and open up to others. "For me, I'd say the biggest part of caring for your mental health is not trying to just brush off or suppress things that come to you, but learn to recognize and allow them. I feel like for my whole life, this is what I would do," she discovered. "I now feel comfortable speaking about the things that bother me with my mom and close friends and have even set up sessions to speak to professionals about my mental health."

---

Pause for a moment and take a breath

---

NAMI suggests these tips for students:

1. Know you're not alone. NAMI reports that one in five college students is navigating a mental health condition.
2. Exercise, nutrition, and sleep are important. Mental and physical health are connected and influence one another.
3. Know where and when to seek help and whom to talk to. Learn about resources and supports that exist. Contact the counseling center for help learning about them.

4. Understand your health privacy laws. Make a plan on whether and how you will allow your school to share information with your family or a trusted adult.

5. Know your warning signs. Listen to your body to know when you are getting overwhelmed or reaching a point when you need to pause and make a plan or reach out to a counselor, parent, or good friend for help. Common warning signs include:

   a. Feeling sad or withdrawn for two or more weeks
   b. Severe, uncontrollable risk-taking behaviors
   c. Sudden, overwhelming fear for no reason
   d. Not eating or throwing up for weight loss
   e. Seeing, hearing, or believing things that aren't real
   f. Repeated and excessive use of alcohol or drugs
   g. Drastic changes in mood, behavior, personality, or sleeping habits
   h. Extreme difficulty concentrating or staying still
   i. Intense worries or fears that get in the way of daily activities
   j. Trying to harm one's self or planning to do so

**Reflect**

1.  What does mental health mean to you?

2.  How do/can you care for your mental health?

3.  What are things you do/can do when you're starting to feel overwhelmed?

4.  Try it: try one of the strategies listed in this section and reflect on what you noticed. Practice first in a moment that isn't charged.

5.  Poetry Connection: what theme is portrayed in Naomi Shihab Nye's poem "Shoulders?" How might this relate to mental health? To what extent do you agree or disagree?

6.  Plan ahead: what might you do when you notice a mental health challenge arising for yourself or a friend?

## 3.4 School and Community Lens: Trauma-Sensitive Instruction

It was just a couple weeks into the semester of my mindfulness course when Eric, a sophomore psychology major, let me know he was working on processing a trauma. In our time together, we had many conversations on navigating the present in the context of a difficult past. By the end of the semester, he had claimed power and freedom to know who he was separate from the trauma, and that he can choose how to frame his life, rather than being dictated by it.

Eric is not alone. The CDC estimates that nearly two-thirds of adults surveyed across 25 states had experienced at least one type of traumatic adverse childhood experience (ACE), including violence, neglect, abuse, or death of a family member. This can impact the health, well-being, and opportunity of youth in school and life.

Trauma-sensitive instruction is increasingly practiced in K–12 classrooms to create safe spaces for students that acknowledge the challenges they've overcome. I wasn't quite sure how this would translate into a university classroom, but I knew that just because students graduated high school, didn't mean they didn't still need individual care and attention in navigating life.

---

Pause for a moment and take a breath

---

I found the following elements to be helpful in creating a trauma-sensitive environment in my high school and university classrooms:

1. *Build relationships*: some students may feel alone in navigating life. A caring adult who knows their name, checks in with them, and takes the time to get to know them can be a valuable resource as they navigate difficulties.
2. *Create community*: structuring opportunities for students to dialogue with each other around relevant topics creates connection and community. Group projects build a sense of togetherness in a shared goal. "One thing that I do like is that we continue to send messages in our group chat outside of class," reflected Amelia, an international student. "We've all been very supportive of each and do our best to keep each other accountable in our social relationships."
3. *Safe spaces*: classrooms can be safe spaces where students feel like their voice matters and that what they have to say is important. Feelings are validated and normalized, and students can be held up by the class as they navigate experiences. "It is a safe place for sharing experiences," reflected a student in a mid-semester evaluation. "I feel like we all gain insight into different perspectives and experiences, and it's nice to hear how my peer's practices are going. I also like that everyone is comfortable with being open and trying new things."

4.  *Hold space*: when students share about the challenges they are going through, it is an opportunity to see, hear, and understand them. Rather than responding with "tough luck," it can be helpful to take a moment to hold space for their experience, ask questions, and make the effort to see things from their perspective. Following up by asking "is everything ok now?" or "is there anything I can do to support you?" or "how are you holding up today?" can go a long way in helping students feel safe and cared for.

5.  *Open dialogue*: keeping an open dialogue helps students know that someone will be checking in with them on a regular basis to see how they are doing. This can happen through asking questions, following up, and assuring students that someone is there for them.

6.  *Resilience stories*: each student has a resilience story of overcoming challenges. Giving them opportunities to share their stories can be an empowering and bonding source of strength.

7.  *Teach coping strategies*: explicitly teach strategies to deal with difficulties, such as taking a few deep breaths. The STOP technique (Stop, Take a breath, Observe, Proceed) can help students take a moment to pause and breathe in the busyness of school and life.

One day after class, Eric shared that his therapist advised that he try to distance himself from identifying with the trauma, but he wasn't exactly sure what that meant and asked for my help. We discussed what elements contribute to a person's identity and explored the question of what role he wants the trauma to play in his life. "My traumas are not me and I am not these traumas. My past doesn't define who I am. But my past has certainly shaped who I am today. My pain has cracked my heart open wide," Eric reflected in a journal entry after our conversation. "There is so much more to me. I am much more than pain."

It should be noted that teachers are not trained therapists, and students should seek help outside of class when needed. At the same time, it is up to those who work in schools to create positive, supportive environments for students to feel safe, comfortable, and cared for.

# Reflect

1. What does trauma-sensitive teaching and learning mean to you? How might it be useful?

2. What challenges and difficult experiences are being held by students in your school or community organization? How might they impact their capacity to thrive?

3. What strategies and techniques might you try in the classroom to help students cope with trauma?

4.  What additional professional development is needed for you to feel comfortable and skilled to apply trauma-sensitive teaching techniques?

5.  Extended Study: view Brené Brown's Ted Talk "The Power of Vulnerability" and reflect on her message. Where might armor or vulnerability show up in your life? To what extent do you believe vulnerability to be a strength?

## MODULE 3 MEDITATION: RAIN TECHNIQUE FOR WORKING WITH EMOTIONS

As you take a comfortable seated position,
allow your breath to move through your body,
inviting your body to settle into this moment.

Notice where your feet make contact with the ground underneath you.
Bring to mind a calming place in nature—ocean, mountains, forest—
or a supportive and kind person or pet to visualize here with you.
As we work with emotions, this can be a resource to return to at any time.

Now bring to mind an emotion that is present for you, or one that has come up for
you lately.
If no emotion is or was present, just stay with the breath.
If one is present, notice it,
welcome it,
trust that the heart is big enough to hold it all.

Recognize the emotion and label it.
What is it that I'm feeling?
With curiosity and nonjudgment.

Allow the emotion,
without pushing it away
or trying to make it anything other than what it is.
Accept that the emotion is present.

Know that you can turn to your resource of your place, person, or pet at any time.
Investigate
with curious awareness,
sense where the emotion might be felt the body—head, throat, chest, abdomen?
How does it feel?
Expansive or contractive? Heavy or light? Hot or cool? Moving fast or slow?
Patiently noticing.

Perhaps bring to mind the opposite emotion,
sensing where it might be in the body,
what qualities it might have.
Expansive or contractive? Heavy or light? Hot or cool? Moving fast or slow?

Now hold them both side by side.
without taking them too personally.
Remembering that we are not our emotions—
they don't define who we are.
Nurture and hold whatever arises with kindness and patience.

Bring your attention back to your breath,
allow the breath to move freely through your body.
Gently open your eyes and take in the space around you.

**Module Reflection Form**

**Module 3: Heart**

Name_____

Date/Weeks _____

1. *Meditation Log*:

| | Monday | Tuesday | Wednesday | Thursday | Friday | Saturday | Sunday |
|---|---|---|---|---|---|---|---|
| Initials; Minutes or Info | | | | | | | |
| | Monday | Tuesday | Wednesday | Thursday | Friday | Saturday | Sunday |
| | | | | | | | |

2. *Meditation Reflection*: how did your practice go? What came up for you/what did you notice in working with emotions?

3. *Workbook Response*: include 2–3 responses from reflection questions in Module 3. Include the question.

4.  *Midpoint Check-in*: how is your practice going for you so far? What's working? What's not working? What would you like to learn more about?

5.  *Share*: Mindfulness in Daily Life: How is your individual strategy going? What are your next steps?

6.  *Questions*: (Optional)

# Bibliography

American Psychological Association. (2013). College students' mental health is a growing concern, survey finds. *American Psychological Association, 44*(6), 13.

Aristotle. (1999). Doctrine of the mean. In M. Otswald (Trans.), *Nichomachean ethics*. Upper Saddle River: Pearson Education. (Original work published ca. 340 BCE).

Barrett, L. F. (2017). How emotions are made: The secret life of the brain. New York: Houghton Mifflin Harcourt.

Bianco, M.W., & Officer, R. (1975). *The velveteen rabbit*. New York: Avon Books. (Original work published 1922).

Brach, T. (2003). *True refuge: Finding peace and freedom in your own awakened heart*. New York: Bantam Press Books.

Brach, T. (2004). *Radical acceptance: Embracing your life with the heart of the Buddha*. New York: Bantam Press Books.

Brown, B. (2013). *Daring greatly: How the courage to be vulnerable transforms the way we live, love, parent and lead*. New York: Avery.

Brown, B. (2010, June). The power of vulnerability. *TED: Ideas Worth Spreading*. Retrieved from https://www.ted.com/talks/brene_brown_the_power_of_vulnerability?language=en

Bryant, F.B., & Veroff, J. (2007). *Savoring: A new model of positive experience*. Mahwah: Lawrence Erlbaum Associates.

CDC. (2019). *Adverse childhood experiences*. Retrieved from www.cdc.gov/violence prevention/childabuseandneglect/acestudy/index.html

Ferguson, G. (2010). *Natural wakefulness: Discovering the wisdom we were born with*. Boston: Shambhala.

Felitti, V.J. (2002). The relation between adverse childhood experiences and adult health: Turning gold into lead. *Permanente Journal, 6*(1), 44–47.

Frankl, V.E. (2006). *Man's search for meaning*. Boston: Beacon Press. (Original work published 1946).

Gable, S.L., Gonzaga, G.C., & Strachman, A. (2006). Will you be there for me when things go right? Supportive responses to positive event disclosures. *Journal of Personality and Social Psychology, 91*(5), 904–917.

Germer, C.K. (2009). *The mindful path to self-compassion: Freeing yourself from destructive thoughts and emotions*. New York: Guilford Press.

Goldstein, J. (2003). *Insight meditation: The practice of freedom*. Boulder: Shambhala Classics.

Goldstein, J. (2016). *Mindfulness: A practical guide to awakening*. Boulder: Sounds True.

Hanh, T.N. (2008). *The art of power*. New York: Harper One.

Jennings, P.A. (2018). *The trauma-sensitive classroom: Building resilience with compassionate teaching*. New York: W.W. Norton & Company.

Kornfield, J. (2017). *No time like the present: Finding freedom, love, and joy right where you are*. New York: Atria Books.

Lyubomirsky, S., Sheldon, K.M., & Schkade, D. (2005). Pursuing happiness: The architecture of sustainable change. *Review of General Psychology, 9*(2), 111–131.

Lyubomirsky, S. (2007). *The how of happiness: A new approach to getting the life you want*. New York: Penguin Books.

Magee, R. (2019). *The inner work of racial justice: Healing ourselves and transforming our communities through mindfulness*. New York: Penguin Random House Books.

McGonigal, K. (2015). *The upside of stress: Why stress is good for you, and how to get good at it.* New York: Avery.

*National Alliance on mental health.* Retrieved from https://www.nami.org

Neff, K. (2011). *Self-compassion: The proven power of being kind to yourself.* New York: William Morrow.

Oliver, M. (2017). *Devotions: The selected poems of Mary Oliver.* New York: Penguin.

Rumi (2004). This being human is a guest house. In C. Barks, J. Moynce, A.J. Arberry, & R. Nicholson (Trans), *Rumi: Selected poems.* New York: Penguin Books. (Original work published ca.1244-1273).

Salzberg, S. (2002). *Lovingkindness: The revolutionary art of happiness.* Boston: Shambhala Classics.

Nye, N.S. (1994). *Red suitcase.* Rochester: Perfection Learning.

Taylor, J.B. (2006). *My stroke of insight.* New York: Random House.

Terrasi, S., & de Galarce, P.C. (2017). Trauma and learning in America's classrooms. *Phi Delta Kappan, 98*(6), 35–41.

Treleaven, D., & Willoughby, B. (2018). *Trauma-sensitive mindfulness: Practices for safe and transformative healing.* New York: W.W. Norton & Company.

# Module 4  Mind

*Present,*
*spacious awareness.*
*Calm, clear, receptive.*
*Free from past reflection*
*and future planning.*
*Free from worry and doubt.*
*The mind can rest*
*in the here and now*
*as resistance and contraction*
*make way for freedom*
*in the vast,*
*open spaciousness.*

## 4.0 Working with Thoughts

The aim of mindfulness isn't to clear the mind. It is in our nature as intellectual beings to think. Thinking is what kept our human ancestors alive on an evolutionary level when they needed to gather food, evade predators, and find shelter. To keep us safe, the mind will naturally reflect back to the past or plan for the future, scanning for threats and opportunities. It isn't that thinking is bad, but that we can learn to explore the relationship we have with our thoughts and how to skillfully work with them to find more ease, clarity, and freedom.

Evelyn, a public relations major, initially thought that not being able to clear her mind of thoughts in meditation meant that it was an unsuccessful attempt. Over time she came to find peace with her thoughts. "Meditation takes practice, openness, and gentleness. When we can approach our thoughts with curiosity, we can change our relationship to such thoughts. They do not define us, nor are we stuck to them," she reflected. Evelyn discovered that meditation is a "process that works to slow the mind and bring peace to the body to awaken us as individuals. When I meditate, I now picture my body as a mountain, where thoughts come and go like birds overhead. These thoughts are not me, not mine...they just are."

We can learn to observe and witness the arising and passing away of thoughts without identifying with them. We are not our thoughts and they do not define us, our past, or our future. In his book *The Untethered Soul*, Michael Singer writes:

> There is nothing more important to true growth than realizing that you are not the voice of the mind—you are the one who hears it. If you don't understand this, you will try to figure out which of the many things the voice says is really you. People go through so many changes in the name of "trying to find myself." They want to discover which of these voices, which of these aspects of their personality, is who they really are. The answer is simple: none of them.

This process of non-identification enables us to watch a thought without allowing it to determine our identity or reality. Through awareness, we can learn to discern whether a thought is useful or not. From there, we have a choice of what to do and where to turn attention to next. Rather than unconsciously allowing the stories and thoughts of our mind to consume us and dictate our actions and emotions, we can observe the mind and train our attention to come back to the present. This was true for Mia, who was able to build awareness of her patterns and interrupt her thought cycle to create space between the thought and her reaction. "I'm noticing now that I often think in negative spirals wherein I obsesses over one potential negative thing until it takes over my mind," she discovered. "Being mindful and aware of this however, has really helped me start to catch these thoughts before they actually spiral."

We can notice a thought arising and witness it without being hooked by it. In their book *Fully Present*, Sue Smalley and Diana Winston instruct:

You can be aware of your thoughts rising and departing without being caught up in them—you can have "untangled participation" in them. You might feel as though you have some space from your thoughts. You can notice your thoughts—Here's a fearful thought, there goes an angry thought, and so on—without being identified with them. In other words, you can watch the angry "thought train" leave the station without getting on it—that is—without getting identified with the thought. You can perceive the thought as "just a thought" passing through your mind. You are aware of it, even curious about it, but you are not hooked by it, and therefore it does not cause you suffering.

We can stay on the platform witnessing the arising and passing of thoughts as they come and go without getting on the thought train. Over time, we can learn to get a little space between ourselves and our thoughts. It isn't that thoughts won't arise anymore, but I've noticed that now when thoughts come during meditation, I can more quickly notice them, more easily bring my attention to the present moment, and the space between thoughts lengthens. Mindfulness offers a choice in discernment. We can witness a thought, and then choose our response without getting lost in it. Each time we're triggered and each time we notice is an opportunity to practice this skill.

When there is an emotional charge attached to a thought, it is sometimes hard to find space to see it clearly. In these times, we can pause in the moment, notice how we might be caught in it, and come back to the body and breath. For example, say you got a grade on a test that you think is unfair. You may get caught in the storyline of how the teacher graded unfairly, how you deserved a better grade, how others scored compared to you, how you studied and sacrificed so much, and how your efforts don't match the result. You follow the train of thought of how this might affect your GPA and future. You may want to immediately confront the teacher about it, complain to classmates, or judge the world as unfair. But before taking action, instead you pause to take a moment to notice your body, your breath, the emotions that arise and how they feel, and begin to create a little space between you and the emotion, and even the result. You realize that you are not your thoughts or emotions, you are not your test score, and the situation didn't even necessarily happen *to you*, it just happened. You begin to relax the constriction and tightness around the experience and allow a more expansive space to emerge. From this place, you then approach the discussion, not as a demand, or as reactive to the test score, but asking for clarification so that you can have tools to improve in the future. It is a subtle, yet empowering shift.

Monica found that by observing her thoughts with nonjudgment, she could identify her triggers while feeling safe in her body and experience. "Mindfulness means observing the quality of my thoughts. It is non-judging, neutral, and simply noting what is arising and when this thought or emotion is coming up for me," she observed. "I can notice then what triggers me and go from there and recognize as well what works for me. As long as I allow, my body will feel safe."

When first meditating, it can be shocking to realize how many thoughts are present, how quickly they come, and how easy it is to get hooked into the stories of them. It may seem like there are even more thoughts present than there were before. This isn't the case as much as now we are noticing what was unconscious before. Research shows that directing attention can be more helpful than suppressing thought. In a study where participants were told not to think of a white polar bear, they found that they couldn't help but think of one. In the same way, if we tell the mind "don't think," that is exactly what it will want to do. When the mind wanders in meditation, we can continually direct attention back to a home base—like the breath, body, visualization, or sound. Rather than judging and being hard on ourselves, we can give ourselves a high five for noticing. The awareness is the moment of mindfulness.

---

Pause for a moment and take a breath

---

### Visualization

#### Sky

Imagine the mind and consciousness as vast and spacious as the sky. Within the sky, clouds pass, weather changes, birds and planes soar, yet the sky itself remains vast and expansive, undisturbed by what happens within it. When thoughts arise, picture them floating by like clouds passing through the consciousness of the mind. Some may be light and wispy, others dark and stormy, but nonetheless, they pass.

Diego found the sky visualization helped him not be consumed by anxious thoughts. "I am starting to utilize meditation as a reliable tool for managing my thoughts and emotions," he discovered. "The strategy of visualizing my negative emotions and stresses in passing clouds has really helped me manage my adverse feelings, preventing me from being consumed by any anxious thoughts."

#### Mountain

Visualize yourself as a mountain in that no matter what occurs on the mountain (trees grow, animals live, rain falls), the mountain is still standing, strong, tall and majestic, undisturbed at the core. In his book *Full Catastrophe Living,* Jon Kabat-Zinn writes of this image:

> The image is uplifting, suggesting as it does that we sit like mountains, feeling footed, massive, and unmoving in our posture. Our arms are the sloping sides of the mountain, our head the lofty peak, the whole body majestic and magnificent, as mountains tend to be. We are sitting in stillness just being what we are, just as a mountain sits unmoved by the changing of day into

night and changes of the weather and the seasons. The mountain is always itself, always present, grounded, rooted in the earth, always still, always beautiful. It is beautiful just being what it is, seen or unseen, snow-covered or green, rained on or wrapped in clouds.

Just as a mountain is bold, majestic, and undisturbed by what passes upon it, so can we sit with the same measure of groundedness.

## Water

Thoughts come in like an ocean wave coming to shore and then are carried back into the ocean. The gentle ebb and flow of water carries our thoughts with the tide. Thoughts can also be visualized to form like the foam of bubbles on top of a stream. They emerge, then release, traveling through the mind like a stream in nature.

### Additional Techniques

- Notice thoughts as they arise, neutrally labeling them with the words, "thinking, thinking." It doesn't necessarily matter what the thought is, but simply noticing thinking can create space around it. Notice if any felt sensations accompany thoughts.
- Classify thoughts as pleasant, unpleasant, or neutral. Notice the tone or feeling the thought may carry. Try not to get too caught up into the thought itself, but more try to work with what arises as you notice your relationship to it. To further discern, you can ask, is it useful? Is it helpful?
- Complete the thought. Known as the Zeigarnik effect, the mind is drawn to unfinished tasks. Giving thoughts a visual completion can put the task and thought to rest. I initially noticed that many of my thoughts were either planning or reflecting, so I visualized sorting them into organized file folders of past or future. When I realized there was no need to carry a certain thought, I visualized putting a big red checkmark on the folder and filing it away or that it melted back into the earth.
- Attach a unique phrase to repeated thoughts, such as "not needed now," "I'd rather be free," or a neutral phrase like "the sky is blue" to cultivate equanimity.
- When thoughts arise, gently turn attention back to an anchor like the breath, body, sound, or open awareness, and begin again. This can help to direct attention away from the thought and short circuit the storyline.

It isn't that thinking is bad or unnecessary, but that with awareness we can cultivate skillful ways of working with thoughts so that we are not slaves to them. In this refuge comes the space to see them more clearly with discerning wisdom to act from a place of responsiveness, rather than reactivity.

**Reflect**

1.  What are thoughts?

2.  What is your relationship with your thoughts like?

3.  What tone of voice do your thoughts typically have?

4. What are your most common types of thoughts? What patterns of thoughts do you generally have?

5. Try it: practice one of the visualization techniques (sky, mountain, water) listed. Reflect on what you noticed.

6. Try it: through this module, try increasing the time you invest in meditation by 3–5 minutes. Reflect on what you notice about your experience.

## 4.1  Uncertainty and Anxiety

### *Uncertainty*

Life is uncertain. Will I be ok? Will my family be ok? Will I get an A on this test? Will they hire me? Do they like me? What will happen next? As humans, we may try to predict, plan, and control our way out of stress and discomfort. Hard as we try, we will not be able to outthink uncertainty.

This is not to say that we shouldn't plan or prepare for the future. Our future is built by the thoughts, words, and actions of today. Yet, it is important to notice what arises in the face of uncertainty and to discern skillful ways of relating to it. In her book *Comfortable with Uncertainty*, Pema Chödrön writes, "The central question of a warrior's training is not to how to avoid uncertainty and fear but how we relate to discomfort. How do we practice with difficulty, with our emotions, with the unpredictable encounters of an ordinary day?" More than the uncertainty we face, it is our relationship to it that determines our freedom.

Uncertainty challenges us to let go of attachment to how things were or how we want them to be. In her book *Living Beautifully with Uncertainty and Change*, Pema Chödrön writes:

> The discomfort associated with groundlessness, with the fundamental ambiguity of being human, comes from our attachment to wanting things to be a certain way...Rather than living a life of resistance and trying to disprove our basic situation of impermanence and change, we could contact the fundamental ambiguity and welcome it. We don't like to think of ourselves as fixed and unchanging, but emotionally we're very invested in it. We simply don't want the frightening, uneasy discomfort of feeling groundless. But we don't have to close down when we feel groundlessness in any form. Instead, we can turn toward it and say "This is what freedom from fixed mind feels like. This is what unbiased, unfettered goodness feels like. Maybe I'll get curious and see if I can go beyond my resistance and experience the goodness."

We cannot eliminate uncertainty from life. Nor should we. Would we really want to know everything that will happen in our lives? Change is part of the human condition, and rather than trying to resist it, we can examine our relationship to it. Certainty isn't to be found in outer circumstances, but in having what we need within ourselves to be able to navigate whatever comes our way. Even if there is uncertainty around us, we can rely on ourselves, our breath, this moment to find freedom.

In the uncertainty of senior year of job interviews and deciding what she was going to do after college, Marisol found that mindfulness enabled her to live more in the present moment. "I've needed this time of mediation in these past three weeks more than ever because this time has been crucial to my future. I've had to make a lot of tough decisions and I've had many conversations with myself," she reflected. "My group studies in mindful decision-making has been particularly helpful as I make these tough decisions. Even through all this uncertainty and emotional mountain, I have been able to live more in the moment."

Pause for a moment and take a breath

### *Anxiety*

The spring 2019 national assessment by the American College Health Association found that nearly one-in-four college students were diagnosed or treated for anxiety. For as widespread and disruptive as anxiety may be, it is possible to learn tools to lessen the intensity and duration of it.

In contrast to trauma, which is directed towards the past, anxiety arises as a fear or the worry of the future. Obsessive thoughts can consume the mind, body, and emotions. As much as we may try, we will not be able to outthink anxiety. What we can do is interrupt the thought cycle by bringing mindfulness to the moment and noticing what arises. We can tend to difficult thoughts and emotions and hold what arises with patience and kindness. Over time, this can lessen the grip and bring ease in the midst of charged moments.

Zoey, a senior business major, came to find that her anxiety wasn't due to her external circumstances, but her relationship to them. "I really enjoy taking a few minutes every day to check in with myself and see how I'm feeling, something which I had never thought to do before," she observed. "I've also learned to better cope with my anxiety as I know I can't change my circumstances, I can only change how I react to them."

Violet, a cognitive science major, had a similar experience. As someone who experienced anxiety, she was initially fearful of what might arise when she sat down to meditate. "I was scared to mediate because I have struggled with anxiety and the idea of just being with myself and my thoughts scared me," she reflected. Over time, she learned to trust in her capacity to respond to whatever arose with kindness and patience. "Through practice I have learned to be more patient and kind with myself. These thoughts that arise are okay and normal and it is the way I choose to react and learn from them that makes the difference," she discovered. "Now that I have been consistently practicing, I cannot imagine my life without mindfulness and a meditation practice every day. It changes the way I walk through life and has helped me heal in many ways."

We are not our anxieties. We are not our emotions or thoughts. We are not anxious people. We may be experiencing anxiety at the moment. Each moment is temporary and will pass. It is our relationship to it where we can find agency and spaciousness to choose our response. In a time of anxiety, notice how thoughts or emotions appear in the body. Feel your feet grounded on the floor beneath you, place a hand on the heart or abdomen, and ask, what do I notice in my body? Where am I feeling constriction or expansion? This exploration can help interrupt the anxiety spiral and find space between the emotion or thought and our response to it.

Anxiety is an umbrella term that we can further distil. Is it worry, fear, uncertainty, indecision, unworthiness, stress, or lack of control? Perhaps anxiety is used to counter uncertainty by providing a false sense of control by doing something to mitigate the discomfort—even if it's causing greater discomfort. We can examine what we care about in the situation and what experiences or beliefs trigger the feeling of anxiety. Can I extract what is useful and choose a wise response?

Noah thought anxiety was part of who he was and that he didn't have the power to change it. Through mindfulness, he gained agency to know that he could change the way he saw anxiety. "I have grown up with anxiety and I always thought it was just a part of me that I couldn't change," he noted. Attributing his growth to mindfulness, yoga, and seeing a counselor, he reflected, "My practice is extremely important to me and changed how I looked at dealing with this anxiety."

Similarly, Diego initially thought there was nothing that would help his anxiety. It was helpful for him to discover that all emotions and states are temporary. "I used to get anxious because of my inability to control the future, and I used to obsessively believe that there was no way to help with my anxiety," he reflected. "After practice I learned that just like how my positive emotions are temporary, so are my negative emotions."

Surveys from the Introduction to Mindfulness course at USC in the Fall of 2019 indicated that anxiety levels decreased and coping skills increased as students developed self-awareness tools to manage anxiety. In an initial survey, over half of students remarked they felt anxiety "often" or "very often" in a given day. This number decreased to 27% by week 15, which was notably the week before finals. Being able to cope with anxiety increased in that time from 38% to 75% of students answering that they can "often" or "very often" do so. 83% attributed this "much" or "very much" to enrollment in the course.

Students developed awareness of what they were feeling, which helped them tend to difficult emotions and thoughts. "I think my practice has allowed me to become much more self-aware of my habits and my emotions." reflected Kamla, a double major in art and economics. "I am much more conscious about how to mitigate and deal with stress and my feelings, particularly when I'm feeling a lot of emotions. I know when to give credence to certain emotions and when to just let them go."

Through self-awareness, Ali found that he was able to lessen his anxiety by finding space between himself and his thoughts. "With such externalization of thoughts, I realize that what I have been excessively stressing or worrying about is actually nonexistent or very minimal in reality, and this mitigates my anxiety to a very large extent," he reflected.

As a senior, Claire felt anxious about her future after graduation. Being present in her experience allowed her to simplify and gain perspective. "I was easily stressed, as I am in my senior year and I am anxious for the future. But with meditating, I was able to calm myself, and during the practice, I really feel or realize that I am just overthinking because life is not as complicated as it seems," she perceived.

Techniques for Working with Anxiety

1.  Interrupt the thought cycle. This can be with a phrase like "may I know that I'm free." This phrase is a reminder of priorities and claiming of power to choose a response from a place of freedom rather than habit or fear.
2.  Tune into the senses.
    - *Touch*: notice the ground under your feet or body supported by the surface beneath you. Pay attention to how things feel to the touch. Hold a rock or object in your palm and observe the sensations in your hand (smooth, sharp, fuzzy, etc.).
    - *Sight*: what do you see in the space around you? What shapes, colors, or items are in your environment? Blue sky, nine red bricks, square table, etc.
    - *Smell*: are there any smells you notice? What is the aroma and how does it feel in your body?
    - *Taste*: what do you taste? If neutral, how does that taste? What do you notice about it?
    - *Hear*: what sounds are around you—whether ambient or more direct sounds? What is the closest sound you hear? The farthest sound? Sound from the right ear or the left? Can you notice the space between sounds?
3.  Movement to discharge energy. Take a walk for a change of scenery, do some yoga, run, or any other type of physical activity.
4.  Spend time in nature. Go for a hike, sit in the park, or be around trees or water. Take a deep breath, look around, and notice the sounds of the birds chirping, and smells of the trees or water. Nature has been shown to have a calming effect on the body, mind, and nervous system.
5.  Repeat grounding phrases in mediation. Use one below or create your own.
    "May I know that I am free."
    "May I know that I am complete just as I am."
    "May I accept things as they are."
    "May I trust in my inner wisdom."
6.  Practice self-compassion. Hold your experience with awareness, kindness, and recognition of shared humanity of all those who may have had these emotions or thoughts. Place a hand on your tender heart and tell yourself "I've got you." "It'll be ok."
7.  Send phrases of ease to your mind for working hard to look out for you and protect you.
    "May you find rest."
    "May you find ease."
    "May you find peace."
    "Thank you for your service."
8.  Journal or ask yourself discerning questions to work through difficult thoughts or stories, including those from The Work by Byron Katie.
    - Is this thought true?
    - Is it really true?

- Is there one stress-free reason to keep this thought?
- Who would I be without this thought?
  3 Turnarounds:
- They didn't do it to me.
- I did it to me.
- I did it to them.

*In application:* One morning as I opened the front door to go on an early hike, I saw an enormous spider sitting squarely in the middle of a web spanning the entire doorway—as if to trap me in it. I immediately closed the door and went back inside. I got a broom, opened the door, saw the spider, and again promptly closed it, anxiety rising over how to escape and what to do. Using this framework, I can examine my story "Spider is disturbing my peace," and apply the questions:

- Is this thought true? *No. Spider is just sitting there.*
- Is it really true? *No. It isn't doing anything to me.*
- Is there one stress-free reason to keep this thought? *No.*
- Who would I be without this thought? *Free to go on my hike.*

3 Turnarounds:

- They didn't do it to me. *Spider isn't disturbing my peace.*
- I did it to me. *I'm disturbing my own peace.*
- I did it to them. *I'm disturbing spider's peace.*

### Obsessive Thinking and Repetitive Thoughts

Sometimes a thought may be so sticky that it becomes very difficult to release. The thought keeps replaying over and over again, no matter what we do or where we go. We try to think ourselves out of it, but it keeps coming back like a boomerang or invader. The mind works very hard to protect and look out for us. It may sense danger and try to find a way out or reflect on something that happened in the past to try to make sense of or fix it. When we get stuck in a thought loop, this rumination can be difficult to break free from. And yet, we always have a choice, even if it takes much effort. Sometimes it's a gentle effort, and sometimes it's a firm redirect, like yanking a weed from a garden.

The thing we practice is the thing that grows. Over time, we can shift our relationship to our thoughts and create more freedom and expansiveness. In times of overthinking, one of the following techniques listed above might be particularly helpful:

- Interrupt the thought cycle with phrasing like "I'd rather be free."
- "Finish" the thought visually with a red checkmark, or even make a brief written list of next steps so that the mind doesn't have to hold it all on its own.

- Practice self-compassion. Recognize the shared humanity of those who have also experienced this. Hold a hand over your heart and say to yourself, "Everything will be ok. I've got you."
- Go for a run or walk to discharge the energy with movement.

### Openhandedness

Close your hand and make a fist. Clench and tighten it. Now release the grip, and open your hand, palm face up. Was there a difference in how each felt? When we live in this way, with an open hand, we are neither clinging nor pushing away. We are not trying to grab more, hold onto what we have, or resist. We are simply being with what is, offering ourselves, openly accepting what comes, and holding it all lightly.

Drishti, an international student, found that she had been pushing away difficult emotions and holding too tightly to pleasant ones. "I don't push away the difficult emotions anymore. Or even when I do, I am aware of it almost instantly and just hold that thought or emotion with kindness," she reflected. She also realized that she used to hold her pleasant emotions and experiences tightly with a closed fist. "But I've learned to just hold everything with a lot of kindness—both difficult and pleasant emotions. I have seen changes in myself and how I relate to my thoughts and emotions that I didn't even realize I needed."

Openhanded living comes from recognizing the transience of all things, that everything that comes to be will pass. If we grip the experience too tightly, it's already lost. No matter how much we may want to hold onto people, possessions, ideas, or our bodies, all will one day fade. Knowing the truth of this impermanence, we can relate to each one with an appreciation for them without grasping what we can never always have. When we realize this, then the fear of losing what we love transforms into gratitude for what we have, and we can be at peace with who we are and what we have.

Abundance and sufficiency are at the heart of working with uncertainty. A scarcity lens creates fear that there isn't enough (time, money, possessions, love, etc.) or won't be enough. This is both limited and limiting and prompts holding on out of fear rather than giving out of love. In our culture of "more" and "next," there almost doesn't seem to be a time when we can relax into having and being enough. Trusting that there is enough and will be enough of what we really need takes practice and deliberate noticing to transform those moments of scarcity into the luxury of abundance, regardless of quantity and duration.

Living in this way isn't passive. It takes practice to notice how we're relating to each moment—and even more so to change a pattern that isn't serving us. It doesn't mean that we don't actively strive with our whole hearts towards an intention. The difference is in how we approach the striving and result. When we do not get what we wanted, what shape does our hand take? When we do, what happens next?

---

Pause for a moment and take a breath

### Application: Managing Anxiety in Times of Crisis

Students experienced the stress of sudden change and high alert during the COVID-19 pandemic. Two-thirds of the way through the semester, classes went online, graduation ceremonies were postponed, and students made tough decisions about life plans. They coped with the stress of social distancing, not seeing friends or partners, and fear about the uncertain job market they were stepping into. Some got the virus, some had family who got it. All had to learn to cope with the difficult emotions that arose with the uncertainty and all the questions it brought up.

How long would it last?
Would they get the virus?
Would their families be ok?
Would they lose their jobs?
What would life be like on the other side of it?

As students navigated the collective crisis, they found that mindfulness afforded them the following tools:

*Kind awareness.* When the crisis began, Drishti needed to return home to India. The job opportunities she applied for as a senior were now uncertain, as was her future work visa. Through this sudden transition, she was able to be present with what she was feeling and hold it with kindness. "These weeks have been nothing short of a roller coaster. I hadn't ever experienced so much uncertainty in my life ever before. However, my practice has really helped me stay grounded and helped me cope with all the difficult emotions/thoughts that arose for me during this time," she reflected. It didn't mean that she was calm throughout. "I did feel panic and anxiety about whatever was happening, but I was also very aware of everything I was feeling and how was it impacting my body and my emotions. I have been more aware of all my thoughts and emotions and was able to hold all of it with kindness."

*Grounding amidst uncertainty.* Zoey was able to find groundedness amidst the uncertainty. She tried to focus on the present moment and what she could control, rather than the than what was out of her control. "Among all the uncertainty that has come from the COVID-19 outbreak and needing to move back home with my parents, I've identified the importance of sticking to a routine in order to keep productive," she reflected. Making meditation a part of her routine helped her stay grounded and focus on what is in her control. "Especially given the anxiety I've experienced surrounding future plans and the coronavirus's impact on them, mindfulness has really helped me focus on the present and things that I could be doing now," she observed. "Rather than worry about what could happen and expending energy on stress about things I cannot control, mindfulness has taught me to enjoy the days that I do have with my family and make the most of the additional time I've been given."

*Gratitude.* As she coped with the disappointment of how her senior year of college was ending, Skylar, a human biology major, was able to turn her attention to what she was grateful for in the time of change. "Bringing mindfulness into my daily life has helped SO much during this transition to online classes and full-time quarantine," she observed. She cancelled spring break plans, missed her last season sailing for USC, and the lost the idea of how she wanted her senior year of college to end. Yet through the loss, she discovered, "practicing mindfulness has made me much more grateful for the things that I STILL have –including amazing and supportive friends and family." She also learned to appreciate everyday moments like going for walks or making meals with her roommates. "Bringing mindfulness into daily life has helped me grow in so many ways, and I truly believe that I would be having a more negative reaction to this coronavirus situation if I had not incorporated mindfulness into my daily life."

*Adapting to change.* Audrey, a business and accounting major, noticed that mindfulness helped her adapt to the situation. Like Skylar, she appreciated what she did have, and she reminded herself that everything is temporary. "I noticed that having a consistent meditation practice helped me transition more smoothly to my sudden change in environment," she reflected. Compared to many of her peers, she found that meditation gave her the capacity to adapt more readily to the change in lifestyle. "Mindfulness allowed me to have more appreciation for having food and that everyone in my family and immediate social circle is well and safe thus far. It also reminded me that COVID-19 will pass."

*Acceptance.* Rather than trying to resist or dwell on the situation, Lisa, a health and human sciences major, was able to find acceptance. "It definitely has been helping me a lot during difficult times like these," she reflected. She found herself encouraging her friends to meditate to help them cope with challenges and news that they were facing as a result of the pandemic. "I've realized that I come to accept facts more easily and I dwell less on the bad news. I've learned to live with 'it is what it is' and that helped a lot."

Mindfulness gave students tools to navigate the big emotions that arose. It didn't change the circumstances of the crisis, but it changed how they related to it and to what extent they were able to find peace within it. Though they didn't choose the change, what they could choose was to stay present, awake, and aware as they rode out the storm.

**Reflect**

1.  What do you typically do in the face of uncertainty or groundlessness?

2.  Complete the blanks: not _____enough. Not enough _____.
    How do you relate to them?

3.  In what areas do you feel abundance and sufficiency in your life?

4.  What does openhanded living mean to you?

5. How do you relate to anxiety? What is the opposite of anxiety? How might that feel?

6. Try it: use Byron Katie's framework for working through a triggering thought.
   1. Is this thought true?
   2. Is it really true?
   3. Is there one stress-free reason to keep this thought?
   4. Who would I be without this thought?

7. Try it: in meditation, repeat to yourself one or more of the phrases below and reflect on your experience. You can also create your own.
   "May I know that I am free."
   "May I know that I am complete just as I am."
   "May I accept things as they are."
   "May I trust in my inner wisdom."

## 4.2  Resilience

Babies learn to stand by getting up and falling, getting up and falling, over and over until they can stay up. Falling is an essential human experience. Our challenges provide opportunities for growth, strength, appreciation, and meaning.

When we can extract meaning and growth from our experiences, we realize that we are who we are not in spite of, but because of our challenges and how they propelled us to rise above them. In his book *Man's Search for Meaning*, Viktor Frankl wrote:

> What man actually needs is not a tensionless state but rather the striving and struggling for some goal worthy of him. What he needs is not the discharge of tension at any cost, but the call of a potential meaning waiting to be fulfilled by him.

Research shows that those who have experienced some adversity are on the whole happier than those who have not. It isn't necessarily what happens to us, but what we do with it and how we find meaning, connection, and growth within it.

We have a choice in how we view adversity and what we do with our lives from that point onwards. That is the resilience, the growth, the mindful awareness that enables us to move forward. Roman philosopher Seneca wrote that it is how we view our adversities that determines whether we are free.

> What is the principal thing? To be able to endure adversity with a joyful heart; to bear whatever occurs just as if it were the very thing you desired to have happen to you...What is the principal thing? To have life on the very lips, ready to issue when summoned. This makes a man free, not by right of Roman citizenship but by right of nature. He is, moreover, the true freeman who has escaped from bondage to self...

While we cannot necessarily predict or control the challenges that arise in life, we can learn to develop skillful responses to them. Ellie found that mindfulness helped her have appreciation for the whole spectrum of her life, including the difficulties. "My meditation practice has trained me to have gratitude for everything in life- little things throughout the day, my health/body, my challenges, difficult people, friends, family," she reflected.

Fall 2019 survey data, interviews, and course reflections of the Introduction to Mindfulness course at USC found that mindfulness helped students feel better able to cope with challenges. At the end of the semester, 91% of students remarked that the course "much" or "very much" impacted their capacity to cope with challenges. After five weeks, 38% of students remarked they were "much" or "very much" satisfied with how quickly it took them to bounce back. By the end of the semester, this number almost doubled to 72%. This satisfaction with their speed of resiliency translates to higher confidence and agency in managing their responses to setbacks.

Though we may not have control over which challenges we face, we do have a say in how we show up to meet them. With mindfulness, Nicole found she was able to navigate her many difficulties with ease and clarity. "The past three weeks were the most difficult weeks for me this semester," she realized. Socially she had stressful situations arise and academically she felt much stress and pressure from schoolwork. "My practice helped me navigate these stressful situations with more ease and clarity. I found myself eager to meditate every day in order to help my mind and body adjust to the obstacles in my path."

Resilience training in the U.S. military and programs at universities including Harvard and Stanford have shown that resilience can be learned. One component is examining what might get in the way. Psychologist Martin Seligman writes of three "P's" that stunt recovery from setbacks.

- *Personalization:* Dwelling on the belief that we are at fault for what happened, and this is generalized to our character. It's the difference between the shame of I *am* a bad person, vs I *did* something bad or I made a mistake.
- *Pervasiveness*: Thinking that it will impact every area of our lives.
- *Permanence*: Catastrophizing that the aftershocks of the event will last forever.

When a challenge occurs, we can notice when a P arises. Seligman suggests that we can retrain the brain towards resilience by reminding ourselves that things happen, and they will not impact every facet of our lives forever.

Though Posttraumatic Stress Disorder (PTSD) is widely known, what is much more common is posttraumatic growth, or the learning and growth that comes from adversity. Research on the Posttraumatic Growth Inventory from psychologists Richard Tedeschi and Lawrence Calhoun indicates that challenges can lead to positive changes in how we see ourselves, our relationships with others, and our philosophies of life.

After a car accident on the way to the Grand Canyon in my 20s left me on crutches, I went through an initial resistance period. I ignored the injury and tried to still operate in my old ways of doing things. Months later, after re-tearing my tendon in a yoga class, I had to have a second surgery. This time, I listened and got still. Meditation became the counterbalance to the movement in my life. I learned to appreciate and care for my body. I asked for and accepted help and learned to rely on others. I deepened empathy for those who have physical restrictions. When I was off crutches, I savored the independence. The summer after, wanting to learn more about my body, I enrolled in my first yoga teacher training, which led to the path of teaching yoga and meditation. I subsequently completed teacher trainings in yoga therapy and restorative yoga, learning how to help people work with their injuries. Six years later, I ran the LA Marathon. The challenge that I initially met with great resistance changed the direction of my life and career when I accepted my situation and allowed myself to be transformed by it. Psychologist Linda Graham highlights five ways that adversity can make us stronger:

1. *Increased sense of strengths*: through challenges we discover strengths we didn't even know we had. We learn that we can endure more than we thought possible.
2. *Sense of new opportunities*: difficulties present new opportunities to use our strengths or learn new things.
3. *Deeper relationships*: adversity can bring people together in new and profound ways that deepen connection and shared purpose.
4. *Deeper sense of meaning*: challenges can highlight a purpose or meaning to work towards.
5. *Greater appreciation*: as we navigate difficulties, we're reminded of the importance of gratitude for the people and things in our lives.

Though we cannot change the past, we can control how we view it, how we rise up from it, and what we do with the strength and meaning it offers. In discussing resilience, it is important not to impose an achievement ideology that blames an individual for not being able to get back up. It does not remove responsibility from systemically oppressive responses that have inflicted pain or individualize what is a collective societal trauma. It does not make equivocal the pain felt in extreme situations with the microtraumas of everyday life. What it means is that we are resilient, thriving beings who can learn to extract meaning, strength, and connection from individual and collective challenges.

---

Pause for a moment and take a breath

---

Psychologist James Pennebaker found that writing about stressful or traumatic events can help people process them and move forward. When we write, we organize our thoughts in ways that can help us understand and come to terms with experiences. Visual processing centers see the words on the page and outside of the mind or self. An undergraduate, Harper practiced regular journaling for five weeks through my Stress Management for Healthy Living course. She found writing to be helpful for metabolizing grief and getting a little space between the experience and herself. "It was hard for me to go deep down into the thoughts and feelings I had been so good at keeping tucked away for so long. Although at times it seemed draining or painful, after every entry I felt a sense of calmness and relief from getting my thoughts out of my head and onto paper," she reflected. Harper found that getting her emotions and thoughts on paper allowed her to separate herself from them. "Learning how to create this separation has been one of the most valuable things I have gained from journaling. The distance between my emotions and my true self gives me room to observe it and not let it consume me," she noticed. Harper found that journaling helped her get in touch more with her authentic, individual self. "I have learned how important it is to be gentle with myself and to not judge my thoughts or my emotions. I honestly didn't know that this kind of self-love was attainable for me."

We can transform the darkest moments by how we show up to meet them. In the early 20th century, Rainer Maria Rilke wrote to a young poet, "Perhaps all the dragons of our lives are princesses who are only waiting to see us once beautiful and brave. Perhaps everything terrible is in its deepest being something helpless that wants help from us." Each of us has a unique journey and individual dragons. While we may not be able to determine what comes our way, we have a choice in how we respond and what we extract from the experience.

When we try our best, we know that if we fall, regardless of what anyone else says, we tried and did everything we could. In her work on vulnerability, Brené Brown quotes a speech by Theodore Roosevelt:

> It is not the critic who counts; not the man who points out how the strong man stumbles, or where the doer of deeds could have done them better.
>
> The credit belongs to the man who is actually in the arena, whose face is marred by dust and sweat and blood; who strives valiantly; who errs, who comes up short again and again,
>
> because there is no effort without error or shortcoming; but who does actually strive to do the deeds; who knows great enthusiasms, the great devotions; who spends himself in a worthy cause;
>
> who, at the best, knows in the end the triumph of high achievement, and who at the worst, if he fails, at least he fails while daring greatly…

To be resilient, we must get into the arena. We won't always get it right on the first try. Not everyone will approve. That is ok. Our work is not to be perfect or to manage the response of critics. It is to try with all we've got in the face of our goals. To keep getting up and trying, again and again. This is what it means to be resilient. This is what it means to be human.

**Reflect**

1. What are the biggest lessons you've learned from your challenges? How have they shaped you?

2. Activity: write your resilience story about an experience that you view as both difficult and a source of growth or meaning. Include the moment, how you dealt with it, what you learned from it, and how it impacted or changed your life from that point onward. Alternate option: you may use a medium other than writing (photo collage, art, video, etc.). Helpful Guiding Questions: what did you do that helped you get through it? What personal resources did you draw on, and what strengths did you use? Did you seek out information, advice, or any other kind of support? What did this experience teach you about how to deal with adversity? How did this experience make you stronger? How did it change you? (Activity adapted from *The Upside of Stress* by Kelly McGonigal.)

3. Activity: write a letter to your younger self when you were going through a rough time. What would you tell yourself to soothe or comfort younger you?

4. Try it: bring to mind a challenge you're navigating now. Imagine yourself overcoming the challenge and the wisdom you'll have gained from it.

5. Poetry Connection: identify the themes of the following poems. How do they compare or contrast? How might this relate to how you have dealt with challenges in your life? What other works of literature, song, film, or theatre portray themes of resilience?
   • "Up-Hill" by Christina Rossetti
   • "Still I Rise" by Maya Angelou
   • "Mother to Son" by Langston Hughes

## 4.3 Identity and Social Consciousness

Mindfulness is an exploration of the questions "Who am I? How am I relating to my experience? What does it mean to live in the world?" Identity is a fluid mental construct that exists within our experiences, cultures, dispositions, and beliefs. As you explore the role family, culture, gender, and sexuality play in how identity is constructed, try to hold responses with kindness, curiosity, and nonjudgment.

### *Family*

Our family members are our first teachers who shaped how we initially related to the world around us. We learned early lessons from them about relationships, emotions, and how to operate. Examining early teachings can help us choose which are useful to keep and which need reteaching to better serve us. The absence of family due to trauma or divide also plays a role in shaping who we are. Family isn't always constituted by blood, and close friends and extended family can become our primary family circle. Regardless of our family situation, we have a choice in how we relate to it and what we do with that understanding.

- What role does family play in shaping who you are?
- How might early experiences influence your interactions with others?
- What might family dynamic teach about how to love, create healthy boundaries, or handle conflict?
- How might family have shaped ways of relating to intimacy and connection with self and others?

### *Culture*

Each of us comes from a unique culture that helped shape our values, beliefs, and underlying attitudes about life and ourselves. As we develop mindfulness, we may begin to explore more deeply how we relate to that heritage and the intergenerational messages we received.

- What do you think culture is and how would you describe your culture?
- What is the relationship you have with your cultural heritage and the culture you are currently in? How does that dialogue evolve and differ across generations?
- What did your culture teach you about how to relate to hardships or emotions?
- What messages were communicated through culture about gender, race, or class?
- What is your favorite cultural tradition?

Layla found that mental health wasn't something discussed growing up in her family culture. "Mental health is one of the trickiest concepts for me to come to terms with," she reflected. Layla didn't ever consider her mental health when growing up in a traditional Chinese family in the Philippines. "There is always this need to suppress or ignore my mental state because there's this larger social taboo against being emotional or being vulnerable," she observed. Through mindfulness, she came to nurture and care for her mental health. "It plays an extremely large role in the way I release my anxiety and stress. Rather than bottling up my emotions, I give myself permission to feel upset, angry, happy or any other emotion. Rather than criticizing myself for my failure or negative emotions, I just let myself be."

### Gender and Sexuality

Through childhood we received messages about gender expectations that either did or didn't apply to us. We can explore what those messages were and how they impacted our identity. In the context of increasingly fluid roles for gender and sexuality, we can examine how past messages inform current identity and the power we have to create our identity.

- How do you relate to your gender?
- What stereotypes or traditional roles exist for different genders? Where might these stereotypes come from and how might they have contributed to your individual gender identity?
- What does it mean to have an empowered gender identity and what does it take to achieve it?
- How do you relate to your sexuality? What does it mean to have an empowered sexual identity and what does it take to achieve it?

### Claiming Identity

The fusion of culture, race, class, language, family, gender, and sexuality all contribute to identity. It isn't neatly linear, but rather overlapping identification touchpoints. In her book *Borderlands/La Frontera: The New Mestiza*, Gloria Anzaldúa writes of living at a crossroads without borders in order to survive what she calls the borderlands. She herself lived in many borderlands as a Chicana, feminist, lesbian, who grew up on the Mexico–Texas border. In the blending of language, culture, and identity, to live in the borderlands involves a conscious awareness of who we are and the agency we have to claim it. Growing up raised in a traditional immigrant culture, I often found myself living in that borderland of language, food, values, and cultural identity. I could seemingly fit in many places but didn't feel like I completely matched any of them because I was a mix of them all. In college, where I first read Anzaldúa's work, I studied literatures of the world and human development, both majors pointing towards the questions of "who am I?" and "what does it mean to be human?" Ultimately, it was not one identity point or the other that I was claiming; it was all of it. I could exist in all worlds simultaneously. They all contributed to my unique identity and perspective. Claiming my identity, with a love of all of the places, languages, cultures, and groups I was a part of, was a reconciling of who I was and where I stood in them.

Our identity is ours alone to claim. Though outside circumstances may influence us, it is up to us to determine who we are, how we make peace with our past, and who we will be. In his essay "Self-Reliance," writer and philosopher Ralph Waldo Emerson advocates for discovering one's own unique identity. He writes:

> There is a time in every man's education when he arrives at the conviction that envy is ignorance; that imitation is suicide; that he must take himself for better for worse as his portion; that though the wide universe is full of good, no kernel of nourishing corn can come to him but through his toil bestowed on that plot of ground which is given to him to till.

In tilling our land, or as Voltaire wrote, "cultivating our garden," we can do our own inner work to discover who we are, what actions we want to take, and what we want our lives to mean. The power lies in the choices we make to walk our own path honoring where we're from, where we're at, and where we're going.

### *I am From Poem*

George Ella Lyon's poem "Where I'm From" sparked a movement of claiming identity through our experiences and cultures. In the template below, write your own "I Am From" poem. Fill in the blanks with memories from your family, culture, and childhood experiences. Feel free to expand and modify to fit your unique style and voice.

---

I am from_____
(think back to the neighborhood you grew up in. What is it like? What do you see?)

I am from_____
(think back to the foods you ate growing up)

I am from_____
(describe your favorite things growing up)

I am from_____
(what music did you hear?)

I am from_____
(describe your most memorable moments)

I am from_____
(describe your culture)

I am from_____
(list any sayings you heard growing up)

---

### Social Consciousness

When we understand ourselves, we can better understand others. We live in a community, country, and world of people who have their own identities and aspirations. The passages in this section are connected through social consciousness as a foundation for shared understanding and compassionate action. In her book *The Inner Work of Racial Justice: Healing Ourselves and Transforming our Communities Through Mindfulness,* Rhonda Magee writes:

> Through personal mindfulness practices, we can begin to ground, heal, and ultimately transform our sense of self, no longer clinging too tightly to a narrow and isolated sense of "I," "me," "my wounds," and the collective pain-stories of "my people." We can begin to be able to infuse our experience of ourselves in culture, community, and context with a sense of the valid, often painful experiences of others. And as we take in more of the whole, we grow.

Mindfulness asks us to pay attention and listen with awareness, nonjudgment, kindness, and acceptance. What does it look like when we apply this understanding to others and the world? To what and whom do we choose to turn our attention? When we hear of injustice or wrongdoing, what is our response? What emotions arise, and what do we do with them? What does it mean to stand for something? Why am I choosing this action or inaction?

When we look at our own identities, we see that they exist within the social context we arose from. This can include social disparities and intergenerational trauma. While there is individual agency to respond to and recognize them, this is not to discount or individualize the suffering from this collective trauma. As we hold our difficulties with kindness, we can include the suffering of those around us and those who have passed before us. The work we do to repair and disrupt this trauma can be felt across generations. The work I do to transcend it is work that I'm doing for myself, for those who will come after me, and for those who came before me.

With all that is going on in the world, it can be convenient to look away and go on with our lives. And yet, awareness emboldens us to look towards what's happening and choose how to respond. In his speech "The Perils of Indifference," Holocaust survivor Elie Wiesel states:

> Of course, indifference can be tempting—more than that, seductive. It is so much easier to look away from victims. It is so much easier to avoid such rude interruptions to our work, our dreams, our hopes. It is, after all, awkward, troublesome, to be involved in another person's pain and despair...In a way, to be indifferent to that suffering is what makes the human being inhuman. Indifference, after all, is more dangerous than anger and hatred...Even hatred at times may elicit a response. You fight it. You denounce it. You disarm it. Indifference elicits no response. Indifference is not a response... Indifference is not a beginning, it is an end. And, therefore, indifference is

always the friend of the enemy, for it benefits the aggressor—never his victim, whose pain is magnified when he or she feels forgotten.

Turning towards suffering and meeting it with compassion, we can notice and accept what is happening and hold it with kindness. It doesn't mean pity, and it doesn't mean that the difficulties overwhelm us. Equanimity allows us to clearly see the situation, stay rooted in ourselves, and respond from a place of wise action. In activist Jody Williams's *This I Believe* essay "When Ordinary People Achieve Extraordinary Things," she writes:

> For me, the difference between an "ordinary" and an "extraordinary" person is not the title that person might have, but what they do to make the world a better place for us all...I believe in both my right and my responsibility to work to create a world that doesn't glorify violence and war, but where we seek different solutions to our common problems. I believe that these days, daring to voice your opinion, daring to find out information from a variety of sources, can be an act of courage...I believe that words are easy. I believe the truth is told in the actions we take. And I believe that if enough ordinary people back up our desire for a better world with action, I believe we can, in fact, accomplish absolutely extraordinary things.

When we see what is happening in the world and hold it with compassion, we have a choice in what to do with that awareness. This takes a willingness to expand past our comfort levels and familiar habits and ways of doing. In *Radical Dharma: Talking Race, Love, and Liberation,* angel Kyodo williams writes:

> To inhabit radical as an ideal is to commit to going beyond one's familiar or even chosen terrain. It avails you to what you weren't willing to see, which is the place Truth resides. To embody that truth is to live beyond the limits of self-reinforcing habits, which take the narrative of the past, project it onto the future, and obscure the present, leaving us to sleepwalk in the dreamscape of other people's desires and determinations. It is to transcend the borders erected by pain, fear, and apathy, to discover a new territory unbound by the privileges and preferences that trade freedom for familiarity and comfort but pretend they are one and the same. Because by definition it can never be static; to be radical is to constantly live in the territory yet undiscovered, the liberation yet unknown.

As we expand social consciousness, we don't have to have all the answers figured out. Asking the deep questions and doing the hard, exploratory work is the foundation for change. Awareness is the first step of social consciousness. We then have a choice of if and how to respond, both internally to the thoughts and emotions that arise within us and externally in words and actions.

When I was in high school, I knew that the school system wasn't working, but I didn't yet know how to channel my critique into action that would actually make a difference. I wrote articles that created awareness and discussion, but they didn't result in any substantial change. During my first five years of teaching, I worked at a high school with 5,500 students and over a 50% dropout rate. It was what was called a "dropout factory," and schools across the country in urban centers had similar rates of students who were pushed out of the system and not provided adequate conditions to thrive. On the whole, students of color and poverty had schools with worse conditions, fewer resources, and less of a chance to succeed. Education theory found this to be systemic, ongoing, and institutionalized. When I was learning how to teach and the broader challenge seemed so vast, my mentor teacher told me that we all have a drop in the world that we can affect. Maybe I can't change the whole ocean, but we can each choose our one drop and rock it with everything we've got. Over the years, I came to learn that to create change takes listening, working together alongside others, and collaborating with students, teachers, administration, and community organizations around how to address important issues. It takes identifying entry points and levers for change, building relationships, and channeling my emotions towards action that can have an impact.

Mindfulness offers the choice to clearly see what is happing within and outside of ourselves and make a conscious decision about how to respond. It isn't always easy or convenient, but it is an act of power to choose what to stand for and take action for something important to us in the world. At the end of our days as we look back on what our lives meant, we can see they were made of the moments that shaped our lives and the choices we made in those moments.

**Reflect**

1. What messages did you receive from the following identity points about how to view emotions or relate to yourself?
   a. Family
   b. Culture
   c. Gender
   d. Sexual orientation
   e. Social/age group
   f. Society

2. What is the relationship between gender, race, class, and power?

3. Read the poem "To Live in the Borderlands" from Gloria Anzaldúa's book *Borderlands/La Frontera: The New Mestiza*. What is the significance of the "borderland?" What tone does she use to describe it? What borderlands do you live in?

4. What stereotypes exist for different groups? Where did they come from? How are they perpetuated? How might they impact individuals and society?

5. In what ways are you privileged? In what ways are you not? What is the cause and consequence of this?

6. What do you believe in? What do you stand for or want to stand for? What does it mean to stand for it?

## 4.4 School and Community Lens: Stress Resilience

Schools can be stressful places—for both students and educators. There are high stakes, full plates, and there is often not enough time or support. Though these circumstances may not change, what can change is how we relate to our experiences. This is not to take systemic responsibility away from schools for creating conditions to thrive, but to correspondingly look at what is or isn't in our present control.

Though stress is normalized in today's society, when we stop to think about it, what really is stress? It may be a feeling of overwhelm that arises when we're faced with a deadline and rushing to get everything done, or anxiety when thinking about future uncertainty, or fear when something that we care about is perceived to be in jeopardy. The more we begin to understand our relationship with stress, the more we can begin to see that stress in itself isn't necessarily a tangible entity. It is a construct of the way we feel about what we're experiencing based on our thoughts, dispositions, emotions, experiences, and expectations. Stress is the umbrella label placed on unpleasant feelings in circumstances that challenge our physical and emotional responses. It manifests as a response to external or internal stimuli that activate the sympathetic nervous system. It's a response within, rather than a tangible object outside of ourselves.

When a stress is perceived, the brain's amygdala acts as the body's alarm center and initiates a response to the threat. In an integrated approach, the hypothalamus works with the pituitary and adrenal glands to coordinate the release of stress hormones that include adrenaline, cortisol, and norepinephrine. The hippocampus stores and retrieves memory about the current situation and previous stressors. The prefrontal cortex then creates a response to the situation. Blood flows to the limbs, palms sweat, gaze narrows, and the body mobilizes all its energy and resources to respond to the emergency.

The body is meant to naturally vacillate from the sympathetic ("fight-or-flight)" to the parasympathetic ("rest and digest") nervous systems. Without calming the system, it can stay continuously activated in the stress response, either stuck on "on" in anxiety or hypervigilance, or stuck on "off," shut down in lethargy. To bring our bodies back to homeostasis and activate the parasympathetic nervous system, we can pause, listen to how our bodies feel, and take gentle steps to restore balance.

As an international student, Ali experienced the stress of starting college far from home, in a new country and language. "I was very much stressed about my first day as a freshman, the class requirements I had to abide by, and just the sole fact that I was 8,000 miles away from my family," he reflected. "And so when we meditated during that session, I really felt a sense of calm flowing through my body that frankly I had not felt for a long time."

A study of 30,000 participants found that those who had both a high amount of stress *and* believed that stress had an adverse impact on their health had a 43% increased risk of premature death. High stress alone did not have that outcome. It was the stressor in combination with thinking stress was bad for them that was attributed with higher mortality rates.

In her book *The Upside of Stress,* Kelly McGonigal defines stress as "what arises when something we care about is at stake." She refers to the physiological response as our body's way of mobilizing resources to help us rise to the challenge.

> Rather than determining once and for all 'is stress bad?' or 'is stress good?', I am now most interested in understanding how the stance we take toward stress matters. A better question for each of us to ask ourselves, as individuals trying to cope with stress, might be: *Do I believe I have the capacity to transform stress into something good?*

Our relationship to stress can make a tangible difference in how much stress we feel and how it impacts us. Furthermore, stress can enhance connection when we reach out to others in times of difficulty—and when they reach out to us, seek to comfort them. Psychologist Shelley Taylor calls this the "tend and befriend" response to stress. "One of the most striking aspects of the human stress response is the tendency to affiliate," she writes, "—that is, to come together in groups to provide and receive joint protection in threatening times." Part of the stress response includes the release of the bonding hormone oxytocin that drive us towards social support and connection. Research also shows that connection affects perception of how difficult a challenge is, as we may not regard it as quite as steep when connected to others. In the classroom or community organizations, caring relationships can be a protective factor amidst stress.

---

Pause for a moment and take a breath

---

### Ways Teachers can Incorporate These Elements

- *Mentor Relationships*: relationships with caring adults have been shown to be a strong component for success and development. The need for intentionally building them in the classroom and in community organizations is particularly true for students who have faced many challenges or who may not have many other positive relationships with adults.
- *Peer Relationships*: opportunities for students to form relationships with each other can be intentionally structured through group projects towards a meaningful goal, small and whole group discussions on relevant topics, and community building activities.
- *Moments to Pause*: take a few breaths to start class or incorporate the STOP technique (Stop, Take a Breath, Observe, Proceed).
- *Emotional Regulation*: students can learn to recognize emotions and process them with the techniques like RAIN (Recognize, Allow, Investigate, Nonidentify, Nurture).

- *Agency*: discussion around what stressors are present and how to cope with them can leverage the energy of stress towards building connection, purpose, and intentional action. Over time, we can teach students to develop an empowering relationship with stress and find more ease, agency, and awareness to navigate situations as they arise.

**Reflect**

1.  What does stress mean to you? What is the opposite of stress?

2.  How does stress show up in your school or organization? What does the response to it look like?

3.  What do you usually do when you're stressed out? Discuss a time that you experienced stress. How did you deal with it?

4.  Activity: describe a difficult situation you handled well. What personal quali-
    ties enabled you to overcome the challenge? What lessons did you learn?
    What does this tell you that you're equipped to handle in a current or future
    situation? (Adapted from *True North* by Bill George)

5.  Activity: make a list of what's stressing you out. What on the list is in your
    control? Prioritize those and make a plan of what you can control and do
    something about.

6.  *Activity:* write a blog or article about stress resilience. Include your personal
    experience, relevant research, and helpful tips.

7. Extended Study: view Kelly McGonigal's Ted Talk "How to Make Stress Your Friend." What message does she have about stress? To what extent is this relevant to you?

**MODULE 4 MEDITATION: MOUNTAIN VISUALIZATION**

Take a few breaths to arrive into this moment.
Inhale. Feel the breath move through the whole of your body.
Exhale, as the breath recedes.

With each inhalation,
notice the breath travel to the edges, the borders, of your body.
With each exhalation, the breath relaxes to your center.

Bring to mind the image of a mountain.
Bold, majestic,
unshakeable.

As you breathe in, send your breath to the edges of the mountain of your body.
As you breathe out, the breath moves to the center.

Imagine your body as a mountain—bold, majestic, unshakable.

No matter what happens upon or above the mountain—
animals playing, birds chirping, trees growing,
the mountain itself is unchanged.
No matter the weather above it,
the mountain itself is unchanged.

When thoughts come,
gently direct your attention to the mountain—
bold, majestic, unshakable.

Let your mind rest on the image
with each inhale and exhale.

**Module Reflection Form**

**Module 4: Mind**

Name_____

Date/Weeks _____

1.  *Meditation Log*:

|  | Monday | Tuesday | Wednesday | Thursday | Friday | Saturday | Sunday |
|---|---|---|---|---|---|---|---|
| Initials; Minutes or Info |  |  |  |  |  |  |  |
|  | Monday | Tuesday | Wednesday | Thursday | Friday | Saturday | Sunday |
|  |  |  |  |  |  |  |  |

2.  *Meditation Reflection*: how did your practice go? What came up for you/what did you notice in working with thoughts?

3.  *Workbook Response*: include 2–3 responses from reflection questions in Module 4. Include the question.

4.  *Book Reflection*: What are your takeaways from this book? What most/least resonated with you? How might it enhance your practice?

5.  *Questions*: (Optional)

# Bibliography

American College of Health Association. (2019). *National college health assessment spring 2019 reference group executive summary*. Retrieved from https://www.acha.org /documents/ncha/NCHA-II_SPRING_2019_US_REFERENCE_GROUP_EXECU TIVE_SUMMARY.pdf

Angelou, M. (1986). *Still I rise*. New York: Bantam Press Books.

Anzaldúa, G. (1987). *Borderlands/la frontera: The new mestiza*. San Francisco: Aunt Lute Books.

Berman, M.G., Jonides, J., & Kaplan, S. The cognitive benefits of interacting with nature. *Psychological Science, 19*(12), 1207–1212.

Brown, B. (2013). *Daring greatly: How the courage to be vulnerable transforms the way we live, love, parent and lead*. New York: Avery.

Chödrön, P. (2013). *Living beautifully with uncertainty and change*. Boston: Shambhala.

de Visser, E.J., Dorfman, A., Chartrand, D., Lamon, J., Freedy, E., & Weltman, G. (2016). Building resilience with the stress resilience training system: Design validation and applications. *Work (Reading, Mass.), 54*(2), 351–366.

Duckworth, A. (2016). *Grit: The power of passion and perseverance*. New York: Scribner.

Emerson, R.W. (1967). *Self-reliance*. White Plains: Peter Pauper Press. (Original work published 1841).

Epstein, M. (2015, August 3). The trauma of being alive. *New York Times*. Retrieved from www.nytimes.com/2013/08/04/opinion/sunday/the-trauma-of-being-alive.html

Frankl, V. (1959). *Man's search for meaning*. Boston: Beacon Press.

Fredrickson, B. (2009). *Positivity: Top-notch research reveals the upward spiral that will change your life*. New York: Harmony.

George, W.W. (2007). *True North: Discover your authentic leadership*. San Francisco: Jossey-Bass.

Goldstein, J. (2003). *Insight meditation: The practice of freedom*. Boulder: Shambhala Classics.

Graham, L. (2013). *Bouncing back: Rewiring your brain for maximum resilience and well-being*. New York: New World Library.

Hughes, L. (1994). *The collected poems of Langston Hughes* (A. Rampersad, Ed.). New York: Knopf Publishing Group.

Kabat-Zinn, J. (2005). *Full catastrophe living: Using the wisdom of your body and mind to face stress, pain, and illness* (15th anniversary ed.). New York: Bantam Press Dell.

Katie, B. (2003). *Loving what is: Four questions that can change your life*. New York: Three Rivers Press.

Keller, A., Litzelman, K., Wisk, L.E., Maddox, T., Cheng, E.R., Creswell, P.D., & Witt, W.P. (2012). Does the perception that stress affects health matter? The association with health and mortality. *Health Psychology, 31*(5), 677–684.

Levine, P. (2010). *In an unspoken voice: How the body releases trauma and restores goodness*. Berkeley: North Atlantic Books.

Losse, K. (2016, March 6). The art of failing upward. *New York Times*. Retrieved from https://www.nytimes.com/2016/03/06/opinion/sunday/the-art-of-failing-upward.html

Lyon, G.E. *Where I'm from*. Retrieved from http://www.smithsonianeducation.org/educ ators/professional_development/workshops/writing/george_ella_lyon.pdf

MacLeod, J. (2008). *Ain't no makin' it: Aspirations and attainment in a low-income neighborhood*. Boulder: Westview Press.

Magee, R. (2019). *The inner work of racial justice: Healing ourselves and transforming our communities through mindfulness.* New York: Penguin Random House Books.

McAdams, D.P., Josselson, R., & Lieblich, A. (2001). *Turns in the road: Narrative studies of lives in transition.* Washington, D.C.: American Psychological Association.

McGonigal, K. (2015). *The upside of stress: Why stress is good for you, and how to get good at it.* New York: Avery.

McGonigal, K. (2013, June 11). How to make stress your friend. *TED: Ideas Worth Spreading.* Retrieved from www.ted.com/talks/kelly_mcgonigal_how:to_make_stress_your_friend

Neff, K. (2011). *Self-compassion: The proven power of being kind to yourself.* New York: William Morrow.

Pennebaker, J.W. (1997b). *Opening up: The healing power of expressing emotions.* New York: Guilford.

Pennebaker, J.W. (1997a). Writing about emotional experiences as a therapeutic process. *Psychological Science, 8*(3), 162–166.

Post Traumatic Growth Research Group Site. Retrieved from https://ptgi.uncc.edu

Rendon, J. (2015). *Upside: The new science of post-traumatic growth.* New York: Touchstone.

Resnick, M.D., Bearman, P.S., Blum, R.W., Bauman, K.E., Harris, K.M., Jones, J., …Udry, J.R. (1997). Protecting adolescents from harm: Findings from the National Longitudinal Study on Adolescent Health. *JAMA, 278*(10), 823–832.

Rilke, R. M. (1992). *Letters To a Young Poet.* San Rafael: New World Library (Original work published 1929).

Rossetti, C. (1861). *Up-hill.* Retrieved from https://www.poetryfoundation.org/poems/45002/up-hill

Sandberg, S., & Grant, A. (2017). *Option b: Facing adversity, building resilience, and finding joy.* New York: Knopf Publishing Group.

Schnall, S., Harber, K.D., Stefanucci, J.K., & Proffitt, D.R. (2008). Social support and the perception of geographical slant. *Journal of Experimental Social Psychology, 44*(5), 1246–1255.

Seery, M.D., Holman, E.A., & Silver, R.C. (2010). Whatever does not kill us: Cumulative lifetime adversity, vulnerability, and resilience. *Journal of Personality and Social Psychology, 99*(6), 1025–1041.

Seligman, M. (2012). *Flourish: A visionary new understanding of happiness and well-being.* New York: Atria Books.

Seneca, L.A. (1910). *What is the principal thing in life? Natural questions* (J. Clarke, Trans.). London: MacMillan and Company (Original work published ca. 62-64 AD).

Singer, M.A. (2007). *The untethered soul.* Oakland: New Harbinger Publications.

Smalley, S., & Winston, D. (2010). *Fully present.* Philadelphia: Da Capo Press.

Taylor, S.E. (2006). Tend and befriend: Biobehavioral bases of affiliation under stress. *Current Directions in Psychological Science, 15*(6), 273–277.

Tedeschi, R.G., & Calhoun, L.G. (1996). The posttraumatic growth inventory: Measuring the positive legacy of trauma. *Journal of Traumatic Stress, 9*(3), 455–471.

Wegner, D.M., & Schneider, D.J. (2003). The white bear story. *Psychological Inquiry, 14*(3–4), 326–329.

Wiesel, E. (1999, April 12). The perils of indifference. *The White House.* Retrieved from https://www.pbs.org/eliewiesel/resources/millennium.html

Williams, J. (2006, January 6). When ordinary people achieve extraordinary things. *This I Believe.* Retrieved from https://thisibelieve.org/essay/7/

Williams, A.K., Owens, L.R., & Syedullah, J. (2016). *Radical dharma: Talking race, love, and liberation*. Berkeley: North Atlantic Books.

Valenzuela, A. (1999). *Subtractive schooling: U.S.-Mexican youth and the politics of caring*. Albany: State University of New York Press.

Van der Kolk, B.A. (2014). *The body keeps the score: Brain, mind, and body in the healing of trauma*. New York: Viking Press.

Voltaire (1975). Candide (A. François-Marie, Trans.). New York: Random House. (Original work published 1759).

Yaron, L. (2016 July 12). Helping students build mental and physical resiliency. *Education Week*. Retrieved from https://www.edweek.org/tm/articles/2016/07/12/helping-studen ts-build-mental-and-physical-resiliency.html

Yaron Weston, L. (2020, Fall). Mindfulness in the classroom: Mental health and emotional resilience alongside academic studies. *Liberal Education, Association of American Colleges and Universities, 107*(3).

Zeigarnik, B. (1938). On finished and unfinished tasks. In W.D. Ellis (Ed.), *A source book of Gestalt psychology* (pp. 300–314). London: Kegan Paul, Trench, Trubner & Company.

# Module 5    Mindfulness in Daily Life

*What would it take for us to be fully present and awake in our lives?*

*To be able to hold conversations and relationships with full attention and presence?*

*To speak and listen with whole hearts?*

*To respond, rather than react?*

*To meet difficult moments with acceptance and compassion?*

*To lay down fear and resistance and open to kindness?*

*How would that transform how we live and operate in the world?*

## 5.0  Informal Practice in Daily Life

Mindfulness isn't something that only happens when we are sitting with our eyes closed in meditation. The fruit of the practice comes in bringing it into the world around us. Meditation is a vehicle for training us to live consciously, aware and awake in life. We can take our mindfulness practice into our everyday activities, into the relationships we have with others, into the decisions we make, and into how we show up to life. Annie Dillard wrote, "How we spend our days is, of course, how we spend our lives." Mindfulness offers a choice in how we spend our moments, days, and lives. We can apply it to any situation if we are willing to bring our attention to what is happening in the present moment and hold it with acceptance, curiosity, and kindness. Rather than something to do, mindfulness practice becomes a way of being and living in the world around us. "Mindful meditation has helped me to engage fully with my life rather than cruise through it on autopilot," Tony discovered. "It has opened me up to the wonders of feeling and sensation that I used to be blind to. But now I can see that virtually every part of life has the ability to be lived with passion."

In everyday activities like chopping vegetables or washing our hands, we can try to bring awareness to the moment of each movement and breath as we operate in the world. To begin, choose an everyday task like brushing your teeth or making a meal. Set an intention to try to be present in mind and body of each moment and movement. Take your time. When attention wanders, notice it, and bring awareness back to the activity. Notice the attitude with which you approach the task. Try to view it with curiosity and kindness rather than judgment, remembering that the goal is not to be perfect, it's to try to be present. In her book *When Things Fall Apart*, Pema Chödrön writes:

> In practicing meditation, we're not trying to live up to some kind of ideal—quite the opposite. We're just being with our experience, whatever it is. If our experience is that sometimes we have some kind of perspective, and sometimes we have none, then that's our experience. If sometimes we can approach what scares us, and sometimes we absolutely can't, then that's our experience. "This very moment is the perfect teacher, and it's always with us" really is a great instruction. Just seeing what's going on—that's the teaching right there. We can be with what's happening and not dissociate. Awakeness is found in our pleasure and our pain, our confusion and our wisdom, available in each moment of our weird, unfathomable, ordinary everyday lives.

We don't need to perform or make the moment into anything other than what it is. When we show up with conscious awareness, we can find the space to choose our relationship and response to the moments of our lives. Even as a mindfulness teacher, I have very human moments where I could have had a more thoughtful and wise response. Sometimes I feel like I am a beginner. We don't need to beat ourselves up over these moments. All we can do is our best and try to be aware, learn, repair, forgive, and show compassion to ourselves and others. This moment is the perfect teacher. What does it have to teach me? What can I learn about myself and others from this experience? Can I humbly sit at the heels of life and let myself be taught?

**Reflect**

1. What is an area of daily life that might be helpful for you to bring mindfulness to? Areas can include:
   - Relationships and communication
   - Mindful eating
   - Self-care and self-compassion
   - Technology use
   - Decision making
   - Mindful learning
   - Social justice
       *(Introduced in Module 2 Reflection Form)*

2. Why did you choose that area?

3. How might you increase mindfulness in that area?

4. Activity: choose a mindfulness strategy to apply to that area of daily life you'd like to try regularly for 3 weeks (daily or minimum 3x week). If working with a group, groups can choose a shared topic to explore as a community and may all employ different strategies within it.

5. Future Activity: share about your mindfulness topic and strategy. Include how it went, recommendations, challenges, any benefits you noticed, and next steps.

## 5.1  Relational Mindfulness and Connection

Mindful presence can deepen relationships with ourselves, each other, and the world around us. It can enhance our capacity to listen with full attention and an open heart. It enables us to deeply understand ourselves and others and to develop a kind of intimacy that enhances openness and connection. It means we allow ourselves to deeply see another and to be seen. This takes courage and a willingness to be vulnerable as we set down the armor surrounding our hearts and show our authentic selves. Here we also are called on to hold the vulnerability of another with care. Relational mindfulness means that we tune in and listen to ourselves and others in our shared human experience. That we sensitize ourselves to what we are experiencing and to the experience of those whom we are with. This can be applied to situations within and around us, in times of joy and difficulty.

Charlotte, a health and human services senior, found that mindfulness enabled her to more deeply connect with herself and others in challenging circumstances. "My practice has permitted me to connect with myself to a deeper extent and further understand the emotions/triggers that had previously upset me more dramatically," she reflected. "It has allowed me to remain calm and at ease under circumstances that would have otherwise thrown me off guard; my practice has also permitted me to engage in more thoughtful, level-headed conversations with others, especially when it comes down to challenging topics that need to be discussed."

In practicing mindful listening with another, turn your attention to their words and presence as your anchor. From time to time, check in with your body to feel your feet on the floor and stay present in your felt experience. Pause and take a breath before speaking, perhaps setting an intention for your words. Rather than waiting to speak, distractedly listening, or thinking of what to say in response, mindful listening means that we hear and are heard with open eyes, ears, body, and heart. Notice what sensations arise before, during, and after.

Before deciding to speak, it can be helpful to ask the following questions:

- Is it useful?
- Is it true?
- Is it kind?
- Is it gossip that may talk down about someone?
- Is it idle chit-chat or does it have a purpose?
- Will speaking enhance or take away from this moment?

Though it can be difficult to share our feelings and stories, doing so is a component of wholehearted living. Brené Brown writes in her book *Daring Greatly*:

> Owning our story can be hard, but not nearly as difficult as spending our lives running from it. Embracing our vulnerabilities is risky, but not nearly as dangerous as giving up on love and belonging and joy—the experiences

that make us most vulnerable. Only when we are brave enough to explore the darkness will we discover the infinite power of our light.

How does it feel to share our story and voice with another? To see another and be seen? How do we own our stories and also receive the stories and voices of others? To let ourselves be seen takes courage and a willingness to be vulnerable. We do not know and cannot control how our words we will be received. As difficult as it can sometimes be to find voice, mindfulness enables an exploration of what might be standing in the way of speaking up, and what thoughts, emotions, or sensations might emerge around it. It can help us discern if we should speak, who we should say it to, and what the best way is to voice how we feel so that it can be heard.

### Mindfulness in Difficult Conversations

"I find that arguing with friends and family is inevitable," Jamar reflected. "However, these arguments do not have to take a toll on your relationship if you practice mindfulness. For instance, if my sister and I get in a fight, if I take a moment, STOP, then convey how she made me feel, it leads to an effective resolution of conflict."

It can be difficult to maintain nonreactive presence around people who trigger us or in charged situations. In these moments, try to practice the STOP technique (Stop, Take a Breath, Observe, Proceed). Take a few breaths and set an intention before responding. Continue to bring attention to the breath and body from time to time, and listen for the intention behind someone's words, not just the words they are saying.

My parents didn't always agree with my choices. When I was younger, I initially perceived this as criticism and thought that support meant agreeing with me or letting me find my way on my own. I later tried to hear the intention behind their words, rather than focusing on the words themselves. They just loved me and wanted what was best for me. They worried that I was doing something unfamiliar, which to them implied risk. We were from different generations and grew up in different countries and cultures, so we had different ways of seeing the world. They were concerned for my well-being. I couldn't control what reaction they would have to my choices, but I could control how I showed up and what my intention and response was.

Taking a step back helps us see things from another perspective. Joseph Goldstein writes of this in his book *Insight Meditation*:

> When you are in a confrontation with someone and you are each attached to your own perspective, ideas, and feelings, see if you can find a moment to take a mental step back and say, "Okay, let me try to understand this from another vantage point." This helpful change requires a great ability to listen. From there genuine communication may begin to happen. This does not mean that you do not express your own understanding. You can, but from that

space of openness where it becomes much easier to speak without aggression. If you are able first to listen, already the ground between you and the other person has changed.

The distance between the sending of a message and it being received can be filled with space for noise and misunderstanding. This can make clear and compassionate communication difficult. Communication involves the input of what we take in and the output of visual, verbal, written, or body language we send out to others. How do we bridge the distance with understanding and openness? How can we clarify the purpose of our communication so that messages can be clearly given and received? Broadening perspective helps us better understand where others are coming from. The relationship between ourselves, the other, and the space within which we communicate changes. In difficult moments, Omar found he was able to pause and see the perspectives of others. "One day in particular was very difficult for me, and it left me very closed off from others. I just wanted to be alone to think for a while and refocus my thoughts and energies," he reflected. "Seeing the perspectives of others became much clearer after sitting with myself for a meditation," he noticed. "I have felt a lot more openness and understanding of other people after consistently meditating."

---

Pause for a moment and take a breath

---

### Models for Connection and Communication

#### Love Languages

There are many different types of love and we each receive and give love in different ways. Gary Chapman's five love languages including verbal affirmation, acts of service, gifts, quality time, and physical touch. Perhaps one person sees love communicated through spending quality time, while for another it is through hearing how much they are appreciated. What is your primary love language? What are the primary love languages of those around you? Through exploration into how we give and receive love, we can better understand our unique love languages, communicate in the way that love can best be received, and openly receive from others.

#### Active Listening

Mindful communication involves paying attention to what others are saying. "Seek first to understand, then to be understood" is a key strategy in Stephen Covey's book *The 7 Habits of Highly Effective People*. We can make "deposits" in our relationship bank account through listening and wanting to understand others. In the "mirroring" technique, the listener paraphrases the speaker's words to express and clarify understanding. "So what I'm hearing you say is…" "Did I get that right?" This can be particularly helpful when having difficult conversations where there may be a different version of the story for each person of what happened and what it means for who they are. Listen for understanding and the win-win, rather than win-lose or lose-lose resolution.

### Turning Towards

Psychologist Jon Gottman's research of newlyweds found that couples who were still married after six years turned towards each other and their bids for attention 86% of the time. For those who divorced, it was an average of 33% of the time. Bids for attention can include a smile, request for advice, or wanting to share or show something. Gottman also identified "Four Horsemen of the Apocalypse" that erode relationships. We can learn to identify if and when they show up, pause to notice what arises, and choose an intentional response.

a.  *Criticism*: while a complaint focuses on the specific behavior and can sometimes be helpful in redirecting, criticism personalizes and generalizes ("You are so…" "You never…").
b.  *Contempt*: this type of disrespect, ridicule, and looking down on someone is the single biggest predictor of divorce in Gottman's studies. In charged moments, it can be helpful to pause and think about what a kind, patient, and generous response would be.
c.  *Defensiveness*: rather than defensiveness, try to see things from another's perspective and express understanding.
d.  *Stonewalling*: if you are not yet ready to talk, communicate with your partner that you just need a little time to process what happened—instead of ignoring, avoiding, and withdrawing. Take 20 minutes to decompress and recharge (walk, exercise, meditate, journal) before having a discussion.

### Nonviolent Communication

Developed by Marshall Rosenberg, nonviolent communication involves recognizing and communicating needs—with ourselves, others, and the world around us. In times of conflict, we can examine if a desire for someone to do something is coming from a met need or an unresolved, unmet need. Through clear and compassionate conversations, we can make requests, rather than demands. The four components involved are:

1.  *Observations* (what happened): When I see…/When I hear…
2.  *Feelings* (what arose around it): …I feel…
3.  *Needs* (values): …because I need/value…
4.  *Requests* (rather than demands): …would you be willing to…?

*Case Studies*

How might you address these situations using mindful communication?

1. Jim has been feeling like he wants to know how important he is to his significant other and wants to define the relationship. His significant other wants to continue to see other people and doesn't want to commit.
2. Megan has been feeling like her parents constantly judge her life and tell her how to live it.
3. Janet and Jade used to be good friends, but they got into a fight after Janet shared information Jade had given her in confidence. It is putting a strain on their friend group.

## Love

It takes courage to love and be loved. It asks us to put down our armor and show up openheartedly and openhandedly. Can we let ourselves be seen? How do we show up for love? How do we show up to love others? Ourselves? How do we hold the many types of love and relationships that touch our lives?

Of a longitudinal study of Harvard men that began in the 1930s, Psychologist George Vaillant summarized the seventy years of data to conclude that happiness comes from our relationships with others. "Happiness equals love—full stop," he remarked. Empathetic relationships even correlated with health outcomes, occupational prestige, and income earnings. In Yuval Noah Harari's book *Sapiens: A Brief History of Humankind*, he theorizes that it is the skill of flexible, large-scale cooperation that made our species successful. The interconnectivity of humans is dependent on our capacity to form relationships. As essential as relationships and love are, many things can get in the way of living and loving with an open heart. Over time, we can learn to tend to those parts of ourselves that need care so that we can fully open to life and love.

## Opening

Love is both high stakes and highly uncertain. Is the feeling mutual? Is it reciprocated? Will it last? To counter that uncertainty, we may want to brace, guard, control, push away, or have an exit plan. The preciousness of love may inadvertently make us want to hold it too tightly. Instead of grasping, guarding, or pushing away, we can make a decision about how we want to show up for love. Old patterning can give way to the courage to trust in our capacity to heal, open, and love well. What are the conditions that allow the heart to open and stay open? What does it mean to be available to love? Relationships of all kinds may not always work the way we want them to—and that's ok. It's not about trying to control a result, but about how we show up to love and be loved in the many types of love that exist. We can courageously trust that if we open ourselves to love, we have what it takes to weather whatever happens. A phrase to cultivate this in meditation is "may my heart continue to open."

## Self-Love and Acceptance

We can only give what we ourselves have. The more we can increase our capacity for self-love, the more we can love another. This isn't dependent on others loving us, or on outer circumstances or external validation. When we learn to accept and love ourselves for who we are, we also learn that we do not need to change anyone else—which is impossible anyway. We can then see and love them for who they are. Examining intimacy can begin with the questions: what is the relationship I have with myself? How do I talk to and treat myself?

## Worthiness

Just as a bird is worthy of love, so are we—just as we are. It is our birthright and we can give it to ourselves. Years ago, I was telling a friend's young child the reasons I loved him. "I love you because you have courage." "I love you because you are kind." He replied, "I love you...because I love you." The simplicity of this childhood wisdom implied that love is not transactional or based upon living up to certain conditions or qualities. We can love because we are human, and we can be loved just as we are. At the same time, this means that we choose wisely the people we enter into relationships with, that we can hold kind boundaries, and make conscious choices about which relationships we want rather than choosing out of fear or default.

---

Pause for a moment and take a breath

---

## Attention

How do we turn towards one another and show up with full, kind, open attention? When someone is speaking, how do we show them that we care what they have to say? Attention is an act of love.

Being heard, seen, and understood was sequenced though 36 questions in a research study on building connection. It was so successful it resulted in a marriage of two participants, one of whom made the questions famous in a *New York Times* article titled "The 36 Questions That Lead to Love." It wasn't the questions themselves that led to connection, but the generous act of listening, sharing, and being with another person in full attention to see and be seen. Questions progress in intimacy and are followed by four minutes of eye gazing. A sample of them are included below.

- Given the choice of anyone in the world, whom would you want as a dinner guest?
- What would constitute a "perfect" day for you?
- Name three things you and your partner appear to have in common.
- For what in your life do you feel most grateful?
- If you could change anything about the way you were raised, what would it be?
- Take four minutes and tell your partner your life story in as much detail as possible.
- Is there something that you've dreamed of doing for a long time? Why haven't you done it?
- What is the greatest accomplishment of your life?
- If you were to die this evening with no opportunity to communicate with anyone, what would you most regret not having told someone? Why haven't you told them yet?
- Share a personal problem and ask your partner's advice on how he or she might handle it. Also, ask your partner to reflect back to you how you seem to be feeling about the problem you have chosen.

### Technology

What is your relationship to your screen? As young adults, you may be plugged into technology for much of the day. Technology has the capacity to either build connection or to create disconnection, depending on how it's used. It is neither good nor bad but defined by our relationship to it. What does mindful, conscious technology use look like?

A senior business major, Hazel realized she was constantly on her phone and not engaged in the present moment. "My practice has made me aware of just how distracted I am in my daily life and how my phone plays a huge role in this," she discovered. Hazel's ADD seemed to make her easily distracted. "I am always distracted by my phone that stays in front of me 24/7 and very rarely fully there in things that are happening to me in a physical moment." she reflected. She used visualizations to allow distracted thoughts to pass in moments when she wanted to be present in her body and physical environment. "Mindfulness has made me aware of this and taught me mechanisms in changing this behavior. I have noticed myself becoming more engaged and tapped into my environment."

---

> Pause for a moment and take a breath

---

What is consumed on a physical and technological level can have either a nourishing or detrimental impact. In his book *The Art of Communicating*, Thich Nhat Hanh writes:

Everything we consume acts either to heal us or to poison us. We tend to think of nourishment only as what we take in with our mouths, but what we consume with our eyes, our ears, our noses, our tongues, and our bodies is also food. The conversations going on around us, and those we participate in, are also food. Are we consuming and creating the kind of food that is healthy for us and helps us grow? ...

We often ingest toxic communication from those around us and from what we watch and read. Are we ingesting things that grow our understanding and compassion? If so, that's good food. Often, we ingest communication that makes us feel bad or insecure about ourselves or judgmental and superior to others. We can think about our communication in terms of nourishment and consumption...The Internet is an item of consumption, full of nutrients that are both healing and toxic. It's so easy to ingest a lot in just a few minutes online. This doesn't mean you shouldn't use the internet, but you should be conscious of what you are reading and watching...

Nourishing and healing communication is the food of our relationships. Sometimes one cruel utterance can make the other person suffer for many years, and we will suffer for many years too. In a state of anger or fear, we may say something that can be poisonous and destructive. If we swallow poison, it can stay within us for a long time, slowly killing our relationship. We may not even know what we said or did that started to poison the relationship. But we have the antidote: mindful compassion and loving communication. Love, respect, and friendship all need food to survive. With mindfulness we can produce thoughts, speech, and actions that will feed our relationship and help them grow and thrive.

When using technology, can you be aware of what you are doing when you are doing it? Before turning to a screen, can you take a breath, set an intention, and create awareness around time? Try to stay present and check back in with in your body to notice what arises. Explore your relationship to your phone, computer, or social media—both when on them, and when away from them. You may even want to carve out tech-free moments of the day when you can totally unplug. Again, it is not to say that technology is bad, but that we can bring awareness to how we use it, when we use it, and make a conscious choice about our relationship to it.

In 2013, Nir Eyal wrote his first book, *Hooked: How to Build Habit-Forming Products,* which became a handbook for the tech industry as they sought ways to make technology maximally appealing and addictive. Seven years later, he wrote another titled *Indistractable: How to Control Your Attention and Choose Your Life*. It offers a perspective of how to choose where to place attention and how to make conscious choices around technology. He writes of the value of exploring why discomfort might arise when not plugged in and to look at the opportunity cost for using it. When we use our time and attention in one way, we miss out on something else. He advises keeping a calendar and identifying what it is that we are missing out on when plugged in. We have a choice in how we spend our minutes, days, and lives. The more intentional that choice is, the better chance we have of consciously living the lives we want.

## Reflect

1.  What does mindful connection and communication mean to you? What is the purpose? What might get in the way?

2.  Poetry Connection: what message does the poem "A Litany for Survival" by Audre Lorde portray about voice and identity? To what extent do you agree or disagree? Provide an example of when you have either spoken up or didn't speak up and examine it through the lens of the poem.

3.  What is your relationship to technology like? What does technology give you? What does it cost you?

4.  To what extent do you think technology helps or hinders connection? What does mindful technology use look like to you?

5.  Try it: journal, do art, or express yourself in some way for a period of time (try for at least 20 minutes). What did you notice about your experience?

6.  Try it: through this module, try increasing the time you invest in meditation by 3–5 minutes. Reflect on what you notice.

## 5.2 Decision Making

How do you make decisions? What is your relationship to the process and power of making choices? Young adults have big decisions to make, including schools, majors, jobs, relationships, housing, finances, and so many more. With the countless decisions that ask for a "right" one, how do we choose well and claim our decision-making power?

Mindfulness offers a way of clearly seeing what we are choosing, why we are choosing it, and the impact it will have on ourselves and others. When faced with a difficult decision, take a few moments to pause and notice what arises. Try to deeply listen and ask yourself: how does this choice feel in my body? Does it make me feel spacious and expansive or contracted and tense? Trust your inner wisdom that you have all the answers within to know what is good and right for you. Listen deeply to discern where an answer is coming from. Is it coming from a place of reactivity, unconscious instinct, or clear intuition? Tune in to recognize your intention behind the decision. What is it that you're trying to do? The clearer your intention becomes, the more you can discern if what you are doing matches the truth of what you want and need.

Pause for a moment and take a breath

Research indicates that risky behavior seems to peak in late teens and early twenties, particularly around the presence of peers. Regions of the brain responsible for decision making are still developing around incentive processing and reward seeking. Correspondingly, as the cognitive control system develops, it seeks to balance this with deliberation of if a reward is worth the risk. With mindfulness, we can take a moment to pause between the thought of a choice and the decision that's made. With each choice, we can shape our lives to align with our values and intentions. In his book *Mindfulness,* Joseph Goldstein discusses understanding the purpose and impact of our actions. He writes:

> (The) aspect of clear comprehension—seeing the purpose of our actions and whether they are of benefit or not—rests on our understanding the ethical dimensions of mindfulness. This is the discernment of wholesome or unwholesome mind states and actions, which lead respectively to happiness or suffering. There is a Tibetan prayer and aspiration that expresses this understanding: "May you have happiness and the causes of happiness. May you be free of suffering and the causes of suffering," …Being mindful of and clearly knowing all our daily activities is the beginning of actualizing this prayer in our lives. When we clearly comprehend the purpose and benefit of our actions, we open to the possibility of making wiser choices. "Where is this action leading? Do I want to go there?"

Connect values with decisions and make choices aligned with how you want to live your life. What is important to you right now, and what will be important to in the future? What are the principles you want to live by? If your priority is X, will this choice bring that?

Sometimes I frame a choice into a yes/no question to myself and listen for an answer. I listen for the tone, certainty, and assuredness of the yes or no, as well as its capitalization and punctuation. **_YES!_** is different from *yes*. If it's with either certainty or apprehension, I know from the way I ask the question, or even my willingness to pose the question. If after all that, I still don't have a clear idea, I wait and trust that the answer will reveal itself in time and that the conditions for an answer aren't apparent yet.

For all that you've been through and all that you've decided up to this point, you can rely on yourself to know that no matter the choice you make, you can deal with the outcome with a wellspring of resilience. Whichever option you choose will be right because you will make it right. And at the end of the day, nothing is permanent anyway.

### Mindful Dating and Radical Consent

When making dating decisions, pause to discern whether a choice feels right or not. Tune in get clear on to whether you are ready to go farther with physical or emotional contact or not, or whether a situation feels safe to be in or whether you should leave. After a date, it can be helpful to take a moment to notice how it felt when you were with that person, and if it is in your best, kindest interest to see them again. Continue to ask yourself: how does this feel in my body and heart? Is it kind? Is it true to myself? Does it make me feel happy and expansive, or heavy and constricted?

Radical consent is when both parties agree to a single sexual encounter. They continually give consent to different things in the encounter, and it isn't assumed that because it's done once that there is blanket permission given in the future. Radical consent ensures that you feel completely comfortable with what you're doing with your body, and it means that the other person does too. Both people are in the frame of mind to make fully conscious decisions and they are respectful of the other person. Radical consent isn't hesitant, it isn't uncomfortable, it isn't obligated, and it isn't polite. It's a definite, willing, conscious, enthusiastic YES that feels absolutely right. "I don't know" is a no. The only yes is **YES** in radical consent.

Before deciding to have sex, the first person you get radical consent from is yourself—asking yourself if it definitely feels like the right thing to do, at the right time, with the right person. You are never under an obligation to sleep with someone and you can change your mind at any time before or during an encounter if it makes you feel uncomfortable. You cannot undo a sexual act, but you can wait until the time feels right. Radical consent protects all individuals and makes sure that there isn't a gray area where someone feels or is taken advantage of. It can be straightforward, sexy, and fun to ask for permission. It eliminates doubt by checking in to ensure each person is totally comfortable.

When we own our power to ask and receive, we expand the capacity of our hearts to open. "I think that some people are scared to ask because they're scared of being vulnerable, scared of being denied. Faking strength is easier than owning vulnerability," reflected Cooper, a sophomore theatre major in my Stress Management for Healthy Living course. "Vulnerability can be the key to having an expansive, loving encounter."

It can be intimidating to bring up the subject, and we may not know how to begin. To talk about sex can be vulnerable and can bring up a lot of emotions around worthiness, trust, acceptance, and how we relate to our bodies. It takes courage to voice a topic that isn't often shared, and when we do, we don't know how it, or we, will be received. Though, if someone would reject you for bringing up the topic, is that the person you want to share your body with anyway? At the same time, both people may be wondering about the same thing, and it can often bring relief to the other person when someone brings it up. When we are vulnerable and courageous, it shows an inner strength that can deepen intimacy and make both parties feel more relaxed and at ease. This can lead to increased safety, trust, and connection.

---

Pause for a moment and take a breath

---

How do you do talk about tricky topics? Pick a time that feels right—a neutral, private time when you both aren't stressed, rushed, intoxicated, or in the middle of a moment already. If you are in the middle of a moment, though, it's never too late to check in.

1. Ease in with a sentence starter that cues that you're going to talk about something important, like "Can I ask you something?"
2. State how you're feeling. "I don't know about you, but I've been feeling/ thinking that…" Or simply, "I like you. How do you feel about me?"
3. Make the ask. "How do you feel about…?" Remember that the response you receive may or may not always be one you want. We cannot control another person's response. What we can do is receive it with grace, take a moment to meet emotions that arise with kindness, and respond graciously regardless of the answer.
4. Validate your feelings and theirs. "I understand." "I'm glad we checked in. I just wanted to see if we were on the same page." "That's ok" or "Great." Don't make someone feel guilty for their answer. As much as it takes courage to ask authentically, it also does to answer.

Note: dating after a traumatic event can be difficult, and it may take time to reclaim the body and trust the heart. Send patient kindness to yourself in those situations to tenderly hold what arises. Know that you are not your traumas, that they don't define who you are as a person, and that you can choose to be a survivor of them. Take a moment to breathe and listen to the wisdom of the body and trust it to know what is right and good for you.

### *Alcohol and Substance Use*

Conscious decision making can be applied to the choice of whether to put a certain substance in our bodies—and if so, then how much of that substance. We can learn to recognize our boundaries and set limits so that things don't just happen to us, but that choices come from a deliberate place of inner wisdom.

Mindfulness offers the power of paying attention and making conscious choices. Self-awareness can help to discern where a choice is coming from. Am I making a conscious decision, or is this a choice made by default or habit? Is this something I want to do, or am I doing it because I want to fit in or because of pressure from my peers? Is it a band-aid choice to numb or mask another emotion that I am avoiding? How does this choice feel in my body and heart? The next day, we can also listen in to discern how that choice impacted us. Is it something that is enhancing my life or taking away from it?

Particularly in decisions where consequences may have lasting effects, it can be helpful to take a moment to STOP (Stop, Take a Breath, Observe, Proceed), and make a choice from a place of wise discernment, rather than getting swept up in the moment. If you are going to be in a social situation where you know alcohol or drugs will be present, it can be helpful to set an intention or make a choice before being in that situation, or setting a drink limit, so that the choice isn't influenced by the circumstances or people around you. This allows for what is known as "cold" cognition processing of a choice, which minimizes emotional influences, versus an affective hot-state decision.

As an undergrad, Vivian developed an addiction to e-cigarettes. With mindful self-awareness, she decided to quit. "With the scary evidence of the consequences of vaping staring me right in the face, I realized that I myself needed to stop harming my body immediately. Breaking any kind of addiction is difficult, but I discovered that my routine/practice of mindfulness could be used to my advantage to help me," she reflected. She used mindfulness to change her thoughts towards nicotine and help her make conscious decisions. "The choice of a healthy body and expelling an addiction to something resonated stronger in my heart and my mind rather than a life influenced by shame and fear through addiction," she remarked. "Two years later, I feel lighter physically and emotionally through lifting the burden of addiction off my shoulders."

Only you know what is right for your body. Making a conscious choice is an act of power and freedom. Making a choice by default, habit, or because it's what others are doing takes our power away. We can ask, "What am I being loyal to?" and "Where is the freedom in this situation?" Freedom is earned through the choice to live awake, aware, and with intention in aligning decisions with values. We always have a choice. It's up to us how we make it.

---

Pause for a moment and take a breath

---

### *Tips for Situations Where Alcohol or Substances are Present*

1. Set an intention and make a decision ahead of time about if and how much.
2. Know your limit.
3. Check in with yourself periodically to see how that choice feels in your body.
4. Keep an eye your drink to be sure no substances are unknowingly put in it. Do not take drinks from others.
5. Stay with friends—for both your safety and theirs. Look out for friends who may no longer be able to make clear decisions.
6. Appoint a designated driver or use a ride service.

**Reflect**

1.  How do you typically make decisions?

2.  Do you enjoy making decisions? Why or why not?

3.  What does mindful decision making look like to you? What does empowered decision making look like to you?

4.   What does it mean to be mindful of and in relationships?

5.   What does consent mean to you? What do you think it looks like in relationships or dating?

6.   What are ways that we can work to create a culture of radical consent on campus?

7.  Activity: role play having a conversation about consent. How might you bring it up? How might you respond? What elements are needed for a conversation where both parties feel safe and comfortable?

8.  What is your relationship to decisions around alcohol and substance use? What does mindful decision making in alcohol and substance use mean or look like to you?

9.  Try it: think of a decision you need to make. Phrase it into a yes/no question and take a moment to pause with the decision. How does the "yes" choice feel in your body and heart? How does the "no" choice feel? Reflect on what you noticed.

10. Extended Study: explore the following and reflect on the themes. How do they intersect around decision making? What would Chang advise the subject of Frost's poem to do?
    - Ted Talk: "How to Make Hard Choices" by Ruth Chang
    - Poem: "The Road Not Taken" by Robert Frost

## 5.3  Change, Impermanence, and Grief

Change is a part of life. The sun rises and sets each day. A seed becomes a tree. Children grow into adults. The inhale breath begins, then gives rise to the exhale. Each day from our first to last. Change is necessary, and yet we sometimes cling to the past or how things used to be. We try to predict, plan, and brace for the uncertainty that comes with change. We may resist change and the unknown at all costs, perhaps instead choosing conditions that are unfavorable just so that we do not have to experience change.

Impermanence makes life possible. In his book *No Death, No Fear: Comforting Wisdom for Life*, Thich Nhat Hanh writes:

> Thanks to impermanence, everything is possible. Life itself is possible. If a grain of corn is not impermanent, it can never be transformed into a stalk of corn. If the stalk were not impermanent, it could never provide us with the ear of corn we eat. If your daughter is not impermanent, she cannot grow up to become a woman. Then your grandchildren would never manifest. So instead of complaining about impermanence, we should say, "Warm welcome and long live impermanence." We should be happy. When we can see the miracle of impermanence our sadness and suffering will pass. Impermanence should also be understood in the light of inter-being. Because all things inter-are, they are constantly influencing each other. It is said a butterfly's wings flapping on one side of the planet can affect the weather on the other side. Things cannot stay the same because they are influenced by everything else, everything that is not itself.

It is the temporary nature of all things that creates life and meaning. It allows us to live in the preciousness of the present moment knowing that it will pass. We all approach change in different ways. Some people tend to embrace change, while change may be harder for others. When we learn to accept change, we can make clear decisions about how we want to show up in the face of it. We can look at what is in our control and what is not in our control and try to focus our energy on the things that are—even if it's just our perspective.

---

Pause for a moment and take a breath

---

There are two types of change: those we choose, and those which are done to us. While it may be easier to cope with change we have a choice in, we can learn that we have a choice in all of it by choosing how we receive it. Change can be gradual or sudden. Gradual change gives us time to prepare, predict, and plan for outcomes. In times of sudden change, we are called on to arrive without notice. While we may not have a say in what the change is, if we choose it, or how quickly it comes, we can choose how we relate to it and what we do with the information we have from this point onwards. We can set an intention for how we want to show up and who we want to be as we go through the change. We cannot stop change (and nor would we want to if we imagine life without change), but we can choose our response to and within it.

## Grief

To be human is to grieve. We carry around the hurts of what we've lost or what could have been. We bear the scrapes and scars of a lifetime of loss alongside the gains. Everyone grieves in their own way, process, and timing. It isn't a linear process that occurs in a specific time frame. There is no right way to grieve, nothing we're supposed to feel, and nothing we should do. Instead, try to show up for yourself and honor your own process. It is both intensely personal and unique, and at the same time a shared, universal human experience.

Grief may emerge in meditation as we sit with ourselves and recognize what is lost. In his book *A Path with Heart*, Jack Kornfield writes:

> As we take the one seat and develop a meditative attention, the heart presents itself naturally for healing. The grief we have carried for so long, from pains and dashed expectations and hopes, arises. We grieve for our past traumas and present fears, for all of the feelings we never dared experience consciously... We can learn to open our heart to all of it, to the pain, to the pleasures we have feared. In this, we discover a remarkable truth: much of spiritual life is self-acceptance, maybe all of it. Indeed, in accepting the songs of our life, we can begin to create for ourselves a much deeper and greater identity in which the heart holds all within a space of boundless compassion.

We can realize that the heart is big enough to hold it all—the joy alongside the grief. The heart is resilient enough to weather the storms and open to what it means to be human. Resistance occurs when we hold on to how things may have been, or should have been, or how we wanted them to be. It takes courage to look into the face of transitions and see a loss for what it is. It doesn't imply aversion, resignation, or getting rid of anything, but simply sitting with ourselves, willing to be in the light of our truth, and accepting what is real in the here and now. Loss is a part of life and at some point, everything will be lost. This is not to say that we shouldn't lean in just as much. For the very reason of impermanence, we can learn to embrace what we have with gratitude while we have it. Change, whether voluntary or involuntary, is a part of life.

When we grieve for what is lost, it signals how much we cared about what we had. The measure of our grief is a measure of how big our hearts are and our capacity to love. It isn't about loss-proofing life, but about how we show up in the face of change. Grief is a universal human experience. No one is exempt from loss or death. This is not to be morbid, but a reminder that in the face of the impermanence of our lives, we can choose how to show up for ourselves and others in the time we have.

---

Pause for a moment and take a breath

---

At a meditation retreat, Joseph Goldstein gave me the instruction to be with each breath as if it was my last, remembering that what is meant to grow old will grow old, and what is meant to die will die. Thich Nhat Hanh describes five remembrances:

> I am of the nature to grow old. There is no way to escape growing old.
> I am of the nature to have ill health. There is no way to escape ill health.
> I am of the nature to die. There is no way to escape death.
> All that is dear to me and everyone I love are of the nature to change. There is no way to escape being separated from them.
> My actions are my only true belongings. I cannot escape the consequences of my actions. My actions are the ground upon which I stand.

Loss and grief are part of the human condition. This awareness can propel us to value our time and moments—not just in spite of, but because of this. Death reminds us to live. This is not to dismiss any real and deep emotions that come with grief and loss. We can sit with what arises and hold it with kindness for ourselves and others. After a death in his family, Leo, an international relations senior, found that mindfulness helped him connect more with his family and develop greater empathy and understanding. "This was the first time in my life that I lost a dear family member," he remarked. He found that mindfulness helped him cope with his grief and connect more deeply with his loved ones in the midst of it. "Mindfulness overall I believe has made me more empathetic and understanding of other people."

Acknowledge emotions that arise around loss with RAIN. Recognize the emotion, allow it without pushing it away, investigate how it feels in the body, and hold it with nonidentification and kindness. Accepting the emotion allows some space around it. We can be with what is present and without needing to force the letting go. Take a moment to send kindness and compassion to yourself and others, recognizing that loss is part of the human experience and our shared humanity. This may take the form of kind phrases like:

"May I find peace and ease."
"May my heart be at rest."
"May I accept this moment as it is."
"May I know my inner strength."

To be human is to grieve. For all those who have lost something or someone they cared about, may we hold us all with kindness.

### *Mindfulness and Cancer*

Learning to deal with life is one thing. Learning to navigate cancer is another entirely. It asks for more courage, patience, presence, and vulnerability than perhaps we imagined we had.

And yet, no matter how unrelenting the diagnosis and disease can be, it is possible to meet suffering with the grace and clarity of wholehearted living. I saw it with my mom as she deepened her relationships with those closest to her, embraced each day as a gift, and decided that even though she had cancer, it didn't have her and wouldn't take her will and spirit.

Psychologist Victor Frankl wrote, "When we are no longer able to change a situation, we are challenged to change ourselves." Cancer is the ultimate test of our capacity to sit with what arises around the uncertainty of our bodies, the impermanent nature of our lives, and calls on us to navigate each change with the hope of grace and acceptance.

---

Pause for a moment and take a breath

---

Though it was my mom who was diagnosed with cancer, we all needed to reconcile what it meant for us and were each fundamentally changed by it. As family and friends navigated our individual and shared journeys, we were called on to be even more present, to create even more peace, to seek the good as we met the changes that came. How we approached it determined how we showed up for my mom, each other, and ourselves. I found these five areas to be helpful to work through so I could show up as clear, open, and available as possible.

1. *Making peace with time*: there came a point when I realized there would never have been enough time. I wanted more time together, more memories to create, to do more of the things together that we hadn't yet. I wanted her to be there for my future life milestones and to share more happiness with her. And then there came a quiet acceptance that I didn't know how much time there was, or how much time there would be. And it wasn't in my control.

   I would always want more, but instead I could learn to be present for the moments we had—and do my best to make peace with the uncertainty of how much time we had left. This brought an even greater meaning and purpose to the moments we did have. From this, we were able to accomplish beautiful shared things together.

   There are so many things to make peace with when it comes to cancer: how we lived in our past, how much and how we will live in the future, making peace with god, the changing body, our vulnerability as humans, and so much more. With it all we can identify where the struggle is for each of us, and where we can find freedom from and within it. Cancer isn't something we choose, but we can choose to enter into peace over struggle, forgiveness over hardening, and love over all.

2.  *Pausing to be present*: there is a comfort in doing tasks. It makes us feel like we are at least doing *something* and have some sort of control over the situation. But when all the tasks are done and all the actions are taken, there is nothing left to do but be present with each other, ourselves, and the experiences that arise. I found this to be way harder, and at the same time, so much more valuable than any of the other tasks I so diligently took on. When we can show up clear and open, and be with it, and be with us, it allows for an openness and availability to touch the depths of our connection.

    Before visiting my parents, I would often remind myself of my role that was needed. It changed over time, ultimately landing at the question, "What can I do to create more ease?" and then to the role of "compassionate listener." The days when there was nothing left to do but be present and bear witness with and for my mom, it was the most important thing I could do and gift I could give to us both.

3.  *Navigating change and uncertainty*: there are so many big and sometimes overwhelming emotions that come up around navigating the uncertainty and fear of cancer. We didn't know what would come next, how long each stage would last, whether the treatments would work, or how to navigate health care in this way, and it brought up a lot for us all.

    An extension of the 5 stages of grief outlined by Elisabeth Kübler Ross and David Kessler, (denial, anger, bargaining, depression, and acceptance), anticipatory grief often arises when we try to rehearse or brace ourselves for future grief. But any amount of anticipation cannot prepare for how we process grief. All we can do is try to hold a kind and gentle space for whatever arises and give it the patience and time that it takes. Honor the emotions that arise with RAIN (Recognize, Allow, Investigate, Nonidentify, and Nurture). Connect to the body to get grounded with a body scan. Tune in with grateful attention and care for each part of the body. Self-compassion practices help meet our suffering with the qualities of mindfulness, kindness, and a recognition of a shared humanity of others who may be experiencing similar struggles. It was often what I fell back on in trying to keep my heart open through it all.

4.  *Taking care of you*: because it can be so taxing to take care of another or to take care of cancer, it makes it that much more important that we take care of and nurture ourselves through it all. The example is often given of airline emergency instructions that guide us to put on our own face masks first so that we can be available to help others.

In times of stress, our systems can sometimes get stuck on ON or stuck on OFF. On one spectrum, continuous high alert. On the other, withdrawn and detached. Discharging stress to bring the nervous system into balance allows us to be more clear and responsive to events, others, and ourselves. Though cancer tests the limits of our bodies and hearts, it can be nourishing to allow for some movement, food, sleep, spending time in nature, and taking time for self-expression and connection with others.

5.  *Seeking the good*: though it may seem counterintuitive in the face of such hardship, seeking joy and finding gratitude and altruism can bring beauty to the struggle. My mom's resilience showed as she reflected on the good life she lived and found each day to be a gift—even to the end caring for others and seeking what she could give. This wasn't in spite of the cancer, but that it magnified who she was and allowed her such grace in finding moments and connection where so much beauty was born of the pain.

## Reflect

1. How do you typically cope with change or impermanence?

2. What's a transition or change you're currently facing? What's important to you in it? Is there anything that brings excitement (or fear) for you in the transition? What strengths or lessons learned can you rely on from past changes to help you navigate this one? In an ideal scenario, how would you want to navigate this change?

3. How do you typically cope with loss?

4. What has loss taught you?

5.  In the face of our human mortality, how do you want to live your life? What principles do you want to guide it?

6.  Activity: write your own eulogy. What is important to you? What are the values and accomplishments that you would like to be known for? When you look back on your life, what will you remember doing? How do you want to live and be remembered? This can be helpful for determining personal priorities and values.

## 5.4 School and Community Lens: Success and Careers

Success is something we actively construct when we align our values, goals, and actions. It means different things to different people, and therefore it can be helpful to clarify what it is you truly want and how you will work towards achieving it. When you think about your life in the future, what do you see? What kind of person are you? How have you gotten to that point? Visualize the values you want to live by and what kind of person you want to be known and remembered as. In his 2005 commencement speech at Stanford University, Steve Jobs told graduates:

> Your time is limited, so don't waste it living someone else's life. Don't be trapped by dogma—which is living with the results of other people's thinking. Don't let the noise of others' opinions drown out your own inner voice. And most important, have the courage to follow your heart and intuition. They somehow already know what you truly want to become. Everything else is secondary.

We already have all the answers within us to live the lives we want. After getting a dream job teaching in the Department of Physical Education at USC, I shared the news with my dear friend and colleague, Kristin. I told her I didn't really even know how it happened, that everything just fell into place. She pointed out that actually I've been working towards it for many years. It was true. I had taken yoga and meditation teacher trainings and earned teaching credentials in physical education and health. I developed and taught healthy living, yoga, and meditation courses. I led workshops for students, families, and teachers. I taught yoga classes in gyms and studios. I partnered with health and fitness community organizations and facilitated mental health school projects. Each thing I did was because I was interested in it. I followed the arrows of my passion and they led me to the career and life I have now.

Roman philosopher Seneca is attributed with the quote "Luck is what happens when preparation meets opportunity." I had been preparing for my current career for more than a decade. It didn't just happen.

In the introduction of his novel *The Alchemist*, Paolo Coelho describes the importance of pursuing what he calls a "personal calling" in the face of obstacles. We may be told that our dreams are impossible to achieve. We may fear hurting those we love by leaving them behind in the pursuit of our dreams. Rather than try as hard as possible, we may only partially try so that we don't lose as much if we fail. We may fear getting what it is that we want. We see those who haven't reached their goal and may feel doubt, guilt or unworthiness. After all, who are we to dream and succeed when so many haven't? In the face of obstacles to our goals, we can examine what might get in the way of our dream and stand tall and claim it.

---

Pause for a moment and take a breath

---

### *Choosing a Career*

For all the hours we will spend at work, what we choose to do for a career will have a significant impact on our happiness and contributions to the world. Some people know with certainty what they want to do, and others don't. That's totally ok. I didn't know I wanted to be a teacher until applying for grad school. I didn't know I wanted to stay a teacher until many years later. More than me finding it, it was a career that found me through me following my passion. It evolved as my interests and circumstances shifted and I constantly sought new opportunities to learn, grow, and contribute.

Executive coach Amy Gallo suggests that when choosing a career, it can be helpful to ask yourself what kind of life you want. She categorizes choosing a career in four ways:

1. *Legacy*: what do you want to achieve in the world?
2. *Mastery*: what skills do you want to strengthen?
3. *Freedom*: what conditions do you need to have the lifestyle you want? (salary, benefits, flexibility)
4. *Alignment*: what values and culture of an organization do you want to belong to?

Which of these is most important to you? Do you want a career that is aligned with your values where you can make a difference in people's lives? Do you want to master a skill? Or do you want a career that affords you conditions for flexibility, money, or time? Regardless of the choice, remember to savor the journey along the way. In his book *Happier*, Tal Ben-Shahar suggests that happiness lies in the journey on the way to a goal. He recommends examining the intersection between what you're good at, what you're interested in, and where you find meaning.

When deciding, ask yourself:

- What am I really interested in?
- What am I good at, and what skills do I want to build?
- What are my unique gifts and strengths?
- What are my values?
- What brings me meaning and purpose?

Each person has unique strengths, talents, and qualities to share and grow through their careers. What are known as "character strengths" can provide insight to guide career choices. Which are strongest for you? Which are the signature strengths that are essential to who you are?

- *Wisdom*: creativity, curiosity, judgment, love of learning, perspective
- *Courage*: bravery, perseverance, honesty, zest
- *Humanity*: love, kindness, social intelligence
- *Justice*: teamwork, fairness, leadership

- *Temperance*: forgiveness, humility, prudence, self-regulation
- *Transcendence*: appreciation of beauty and excellence, gratitude, hope, humor, spirituality

It isn't just the career, but how we think about it that contributes to work satisfaction. Psychologist Amy Wrzeniewski and her colleagues suggest that people perceive their work in one of three ways: as a job or chore, as a career motivated by extrinsic factors, or as a calling from which motivation and personal fulfillment are derived. Regardless of the job title, be it janitor or CEO, how we orient ourselves to think about the purpose of the work we do has a significant impact on happiness in work and life.

It is very common for people to change careers in their lifetime. With the pace of technology, you may be working in a future career that doesn't even exist yet. For this reason, it can be helpful to focus on skills you want to build and create a versatile foundation where you can deepen transferable skills.

### Job Interviews

Take time to manage big emotions that may arise before an interview with RAIN (Recognize, Allow, Investigate, Nonidentify and Nurture) and remind yourself that you have what it takes to do your best.

#### Before

- Research the company and align their goals with your resume.
- Prepare to share stories and examples from your life that are relevant to the organization's mission.
- Practice answering sample interview questions with a trusted friend or adviser.

#### During

- Be on time and professional—dress, handshake, eye contact.
- Practice active listening and pay attention to names and what people say.
- Make a personal connection and be professionally friendly.

#### After

- Follow up with an email or card thanking them for their time and consideration.
- Release emphasis on result and take each experience as a learning lesson.

#### Practice Questions

- Tell me about yourself.
- Describe yourself in three words. Discuss your strengths and weaknesses.

- Why should we hire you over the other applicants?
- Tell me about a time when you dealt with a challenging situation or conflict. How did you handle it?
- Tell me about a time when you made a mistake. How did you address it?
- Give an example of when you showed leadership and initiative.
- Tell about the moment in your life that you are most proud of.
- What are your short and long-term career goals? Where do you see yourself in 3-5 years?
- Why are you interested in working for our company?
- Why would you excel at this job?
- Do you have any questions for us?

### Freedom of Time and Money

*Time*

There are a finite number of breaths we will take and days we will live. How we spend our time is how we spend our lives. Each person has the same twenty-four hours in a day. Being intentional about how to use, spend, and prioritize time can help to align values with choices and actions. This involves consciously choosing what is important to spend time on and what isn't and learning what to say yes and no to. It takes learning about our own internal clocks and discovering routines for when we work best, when we need sleep, and discerning what is worth our time.

Both what we do and how we do it matters. As I was rushing around town one day running errands, I flipped through a magazine in my mechanic's waiting room. It included an excerpt from Arianna Huffington's book *Thrive* about the concept of operating in time scarcity (there isn't enough time) versus time luxury (there's plenty of time). This is the difference between "I don't have all day" and "I have all day." A day can be full, and yet the way we approach our tasks can vary from feeling rushed and frazzled—to approaching each task and moment with full attention. After that day, I read her book and I realized how I wanted to see and spend my time. Basketball Coach John Wooden told his athletes, "Be quick, but don't hurry." We can have things to do, and still take the time to do them with attention and care. Freedom of time isn't doing nothing; it's choosing what to spend our time on in alignment with the truth of what is important to us.

Practical Tips

1. Find a system to plan out your time (planner, calendar, etc.).
2. Prioritize and spend the most amount of time on the things that are the most important.
3. Identify when it is that you work best (morning, evening, etc.) and try to plan your work around your internal clock.
4. Do the most important tasks first, when you're freshest.
5. Identify time wasters and distractions. Ask, "Is this worth my time?"

6.  Manage technology time usage.
7.  For lengthy tasks, chunk it into smaller parts and take mini breaks every 30-45 minutes to recharge.
8.  For overwhelming tasks, identify the smallest first step you can take and do that. Identify the next smallest step and do that too. Keep going.
9.  Simplify your schedule to devote attention to the things that are most aligned with your goals.
10. Pause regularly to savor the moment and reset.

---

Pause for a moment and take a breath

---

## Money

Our relationship with money can either lead to feeling powerful or powerless. Regardless of the amount we have, we can learn to relate to finances from a place of courage, truth, and freedom. The most important component of building financial literacy isn't money—it's values. Once we clarify what is important, we can then align choices around those priorities. Money can be an empowering source of actualizing goals in alignment with resources—or it can have a devastating impact if used with disregard for its power. For these reasons, it is important to clarify what you want to use money for, why you want to spend it in that way, and how to earn and save with that goal in mind.

Suze Orman discusses the importance of living in alignment with financial truth. If we waste money, disrespect it, or spend it frivolously with disregard, we are limiting its power. On the other hand, when we spend in alignment with our truth of how much we have, how much we need, and how to act in alignment with our spiritual and material truth, we magnify the power and potential of money to be a catalyst to achieve financial freedom. This freedom does not come based on the amount we have, but in noticing our relationship to it, recognizing our financial truth, and acting in accordance with our values. What we spend our money (and time, energy, and attention) on is a direct reflection of what is important to us. We vote with our wallets and can learn to do so with conscious consumerism about the items we buy and the values of the businesses we support by buying from.

Past the point where basic needs are met, research shows that having more money doesn't necessarily make us much happier. After this point, it's how we spend and relate to money that has a bigger impact on happiness than the amount we have. Spending on experiences or others has been shown to create more happiness than spending on things. Because of the process of hedonic adaptation, or the law of diminishing return, we adapt to our circumstances and to our purchases. It may feel great to have a new item for a little while, but after a while it might not garner the same thrill.

Practical Tips

1. Develop a system for budgeting of money earned, spent, and saved.
2. Track everyday purchases—they add up over time.
3. Live within your means.
4. Distinguish between wants and needs. Set a spending limit for wants. Wait 24–48 hours to purchase a large want.
5. Start contributing for retirement now. This is a necessity, not a luxury.
6. Beware of credit cards with fees and high interest rates. Pay the balance in full, if possible, to avoid interest charges.
7. Earn a strong credit score through on-time payments, paying down debt, and starting your credit history now if you haven't already. Try not to max out credit card spending limits or open many applications.
8. Get informed about loans. Opt for subsidized student loans to avoid interest accruing while in school. Seek loan forgiveness programs. Consolidate and refinance if it will be advantageous. Look into a loan repayment program.
9. For happiness, spend on experiences and others, rather than things. Spend on a future purchase (like a vacation within your means) to have something to look forward to.
10. Aim for 6–8 months of savings in case of an emergency or a change in circumstances.

## *Mindful Meetings*

Mindfulness can help meetings be more intentional, efficient, and aligned. We can explore our relationship to them and the conscious or unconscious roles we play in them. Strategies for incorporating mindfulness into meetings include:

1.  *Set an intention*: what is the purpose of the meeting? Is a meeting necessary to achieve the purpose? Align the purpose of the meeting with the purpose and vision of the organization.
2.  *Choose a platform*: what is the best platform to achieve the desired goals? In person or virtual? Is a meeting necessary to achieve this goal?
3.  *Welcome everyone to the space*: show participants they are important and belong there.
4.  *Take a few breaths*: acknowledge that people may have come in carrying stress from the day. Take a moment to pause to come together before diving into content. This will create a calmer, more receptive space.
5.  *Create shared norms*: what are the conditions individuals need from the group to feel safe, heard, understood, and productive?
6.  *Manage group emotions*: keep a pulse on the room to notice what emotions seem to arise around receiving certain news, comments, or projects. Adjust plans as needed.
7.  *Equity in voice*: what is the protocol for sharing and hearing voices?
8.  *Feedback mechanisms*: how is feedback given? What are the mechanisms by which feedback is collected? What is done with it?
9.  *Decision-making processes*: how are decisions made? Unilaterally? By majority? Consensus? What type of decision-making process best aligns with meeting objectives and organization's vision?
10. *Notice power dynamics*: are there a few people who generally speak and make decisions for the group? How does this impact the investment and ownership of the team? To what extent are power, race, class, gender, or sexuality dynamics explicitly or implicitly showing up?
11. *Takeaways and next steps*: what are the takeaways and next steps? Who will be doing them? Why those people? By when? For what end?
12. *Closing breath*: close with a few breaths to honor everyone's time and contributions.

---

Pause for a moment and take a breath

---

**Reflect**

1. What does success look like to you? When does it happen? Under what circumstances? What might get in the way of success? How do you know when you're successful?

2a. Fill in the Blanks:
   - Professional success is to me…

   - Financial success is to me…

   - Interpersonal/relational success is to me…

   - Physical and mental health success is to me…

   - Happiness is to me…

2b. Rank them according to which you value most. Why did you order them in that way?

3.  What do you really want to do for a career? What brings you meaning and purpose? What are your unique gifts and strengths?

4.  Activity: interview someone you think is successful. Reflect on your experience. What shaped their choices in life? What is their life philosophy? What most surprised you?

5.  Activity: read Paolo Coelho's introduction to *The Alchemist*. What does he mean by "personal calling?" How might the four obstacles get in the way of a dream and what can be done in the face of them?

6.  How can mindfulness be used in job interviews?

7.  Activity: practice interviewing for a job with someone. Reflect on how it went and next steps.

8.  How might mindfulness apply to your major or career?

9.  What do you currently spend your time on? What are your highest priorities and values? What gets in the way of spending time on the things you value most? Make a plan of how you want to spend your time.

10. What does financial freedom mean to you? What is your relationship with money like? What are your values when it comes to money? Make a financial plan to manage saving, earning, and spending.

**MODULE 5 MEDITATION: DECISION MAKING**

Take few breaths to arrive into this moment.
The inhale begins and ends.
The exhale begins and ends.
Notice the space between the inhale and exhale.

Trust the cycle of the breath;
it knows just what to do.
Trust that you have what it takes to navigate this moment.

Bring to mind a decision you are in the process of making.
Phrase it into a yes or no question.

Choose yes for your decision.
Notice how the "yes" feels in your body.
Is it expansive or contractive, heavy or light, open or closed?
Is it a bold capitalized **YES**, or lowercase yes?
Try to hold what arises with curiosity, nonjudgment, and patience.

Now notice how the "no" feels.
Is it expansive or contractive, heavy or light, open or closed?
Is it a bold capital **NO**, or lowercase no?
With curiosity, nonjudgment, and patience.

Hold them both side by side.
Simply sensing with awareness,

let the yes and no fall away.

Trust that you have what it takes to make your best choice.
Trust that it will be ok no matter what.
Notice what arises.
Sense the boldness of making a decision.

Take another breath in.
Exhale.

**Module Reflection Form**

**Module 5: Mindfulness in Daily Life**

Name_____

Date/Weeks _____

1.  *Meditation Log.*

|  | Monday | Tuesday | Wednesday | Thursday | Friday | Saturday | Sunday |
|---|---|---|---|---|---|---|---|
| Initials; Minutes or Info |  |  |  |  |  |  |  |
|  | Monday | Tuesday | Wednesday | Thursday | Friday | Saturday | Sunday |
|  |  |  |  |  |  |  |  |
|  | Monday | Tuesday | Wednesday | Thursday | Friday | Saturday | Sunday |
|  |  |  |  |  |  |  |  |

2.  *Meditation Reflection*: how did your practice go? What came up for you/what did you notice in applying mindfulness to daily life?

3.  *Workbook Response*: include 2–3 responses from reflection questions in Module 5. Include the question.

4.  *Mindfulness in Daily Life Reflection*: how did your strategy go? Include how long you practiced it, challenges, benefits, and next steps.

5.  *Meditation Class*: take a meditation class. Where/when did you attend? How did it go? What did you notice?

6.  *Impact*: how has your practice impacted you overall? What are your strengths, challenges, and next steps?

7.  *Questions*: (Optional)

# Bibliography

Aron, A., Melinat, E., Aron, E.N., Vallone, R.D., & Bator, R.J. (1997). The experimental generation of interpersonal closeness: A procedure and some preliminary findings. *Personality and Social Psychology Bulletin, 23*(4), 363–377.

Ben-Shahar, T. (2007). *Happier: Learn secrets to daily joy and lasting fulfillment.* New York: McGraw-Hill Education.

Bennet, J., & Jones, D. (2018, May 5). 45 stories of sex and consent on campus. *New York Times.* Retrieved from http://www.nytimes.com/interactive/2018/05/10/style/sexual-consent-college-campus.html

Brown, B. (2013). *Daring greatly: How the courage to be vulnerable transforms the way we live, love, parent and lead.* New York: Avery.

Chang, R. (2014, May). How to make hard choices. *TED: Ideas Worth Spreading.* Retrieved from https://www.ted.com/talks/ruth_chang_how:to_make_hard_choices?language=en

Chapman, G.D. (1995). *The five love languages: How to express heartfelt commitment to your mate.* Chicago: Northfield Publishing.

Chein, J., Albert, D., O'Brien, L., Uckert, K., & Steinberg, L. (2011). Peers increase adolescent risk taking by enhancing activity in the brain's reward circuitry. *Developmental Science, 14*(2), F1–F10.

Chödrön, P. (2000). *When things fall apart.* Boston: Shambhala Classics.

Coelho, P. (1993). *The alchemist.* New York: Harper Collins.

Covey, S.R. (2004). *The 7 habits of highly effective people: Restoring the character ethic.* New York: Free Press.

Eyal, N. (2014). *Hooked: How to build habit-forming products.* New York: Portfolio / Penguin.

Eyal, N. (2019). *Indistractable: How to control your attention and choose your life.* Dallas: BenBella Books.

Frost, R., & Untermeyer, L. (1991). *The road not taken: A selection of Robert Frost's poems.* New York: H. Holt and Company. (Original work published 1916).

Gallo, A. (2015, February 4). How to build a meaningful career. *Harvard Business Review.* Retrieved from https://hbr.org/2015/02/how-to-build-a-meaningful-career

Goldstein, J. (2003). *Insight meditation: The practice of freedom.* Boulder: Shambhala Classics.

Goldstein, J. (2016). *Mindfulness: A practical guide to awakening.* Boulder: Sounds True.

Gottman, J.M., & Silver, N. (1999). *The seven principles for making marriage work.* New York: Three Rivers Press.

Hanh, T.N. (2000) *Plum Village chanting book and recitation.* Berkeley: Parallax Press.

Hanh, T.N. (2002). *No death no fear: Comforting wisdom for life.* New York: Riverhead Books.

Hanh, T.N. (2014). *The art of communicating.* New York: Harper One.

Harari, Y.N. (2015). *Sapiens: A brief history of humankind.* New York: Harper.

Huffington, A. (2014). *Thrive: The third metric to redefining success and creating a life of well-being, wisdom, and wonder.* New York: Crown Publishing Group.

Jobs, S. (2005, June 12). "You've got to find what you love," Jobs says. *Stanford News.* Retrieved from https://news.stanford.edu/2005/06/14/jobs-061505/

Jones, D. (2015, January 9). The 36 questions that lead to love. *New York Times.* Retrieved from https://www.nytimes.com/2015/01/11/style/36-questions-that-lead-to-love.html

Kabat-Zinn, J. (2005). *Full catastrophe living: Using the wisdom of your body and mind to face stress, pail, and illness* (15th anniversary ed.). New York: Bantam Press Dell.

Khanna, P., & Singh, K. (2019). Do all positive psychology exercises work for everyone? Replication of Seligman et al.'s (2005) interventions among adolescents. *Psychological Studies, 64*(1), 1–10.

Kornfield, J. (1993). *A path with heart.* New York: Bantam Press Books.

Kübler-Ross, E., & Kessler, D. (2005). *On grief and grieving: Finding the meaning of grief through the five stages of loss.* New York: Scribner.

Loewenstein, G. (2005). Hot-cold empathy gaps and medical decision making. *Health Psychology. American Psychological Association, 24*(4S), S49–S56.

Lorde, A. (2000). *The collected poems of Audre Lorde. New York: W.W. Norton & Company.*

McGonigal, K. (2011). *The willpower instinct.* New York: Penguin Publishing Group.

Orman, S. (2001). *The courage to be rich: Creating a life of material and spiritual abundance.* New York: Riverhead Books.

Orman, S. (2007). *The money book for the young, fabulous, and broke.* New York: Riverhead Books.

Pennebaker, J.W. (1997a). *Opening up: The healing power of expressing emotions.* New York: Guilford.

Pennebaker, J.W. (1997b). Writing about emotional experience as a therapeutic process. *Psychological Science, 8*(3), 162–166.

Rosenberg, M.B. (2003). *Nonviolent communication: A language of life.* Encinitas: PuddleDancer Press.

Stone, D., Patton, B., & Heen, S. (2000). *Difficult conversations: How to discuss what matters most.* New York: Penguin Books.

Vaillant, G.E. (2012). *Triumphs of experience: The men of the Harvard grant study.* Cambridge, MA: Belknap Press of Harvard University Press.

Vaillant, G.E. (2015). Happiness equals love, full stop. In S. Polly & K. Britton (Eds.), *Character strengths matter: How to live a full life.* Philadelphia: Positive Psychology News.

Webb, C. (2019). *How to have a good day: The essential toolkit for a productive day at work and beyond.* London: Macmillan.

Wrzesniewski, A., McCauley, C., Rozin, P., & Schwartz, B. (1997). Jobs, careers, and callings: People's relations to their work. *Journal of Research in Personality, 31*(1), 21–33.

# Conclusion

We don't need to be anything other than who we are. We have everything already within us to live a life that is present, aware, and awake. In his book *Your True Home*, Thich Nhat Hanh writes:

> All we have to do is be ourselves, fully and authentically. We don't have to run after anything. We already contain the whole cosmos. We simply return to ourselves through mindfulness, and touch the peace and joy that are already present within us and all around us. I have arrived. I am already home...
>
> Your true home is in the here and the now. It is not limited by time, space, nationality, or race. Your true home is not an abstract idea; it is something you can touch and live in every moment...
>
> We believe that happiness is possible only in the future. That is why the practice 'I have arrived' is very important. The realization that we have already arrived, that we don't have to travel any further, that we are already here, can give us peace and joy. The conditions for our happiness are already sufficient. We only need to allow ourselves to be in the present moment, and we will be able to touch them.

Rather than an external thing to do, mindfulness is a coming home and uncovering of who we are. We can do it anytime and anywhere. "One of my favorite aspects of mindfulness that I have grown to learn, understand, and develop in my own life is the idea that mindfulness can happen anywhere," Emma reflected. "Whether you are frustrated while driving in traffic, on your way to class, or just have a few minutes of silence to spare in between all of the 'busy' that tends to take over our schedules this time of year. Mindfulness is recognizing this and letting it 'do its thing' and then gently pass."

---

Pause for a moment and take a breath

---

The thing we practice is the thing that grows. Peace and freedom can be found in planting seeds to be more present, open, kind, and accepting. Though we often can't control the world around us, we can notice what arises within us and choose how we want to show up. The refuge of practice is always available—if only we can take a moment to pause and open to it. Of this, Tara Brach writes in her book *True Refuge*:

> The biggest illusion about a path of refuge is that we are on our way somewhere else, on our way to becoming a different kind of person. But ultimately, our refuge is not outside ourselves, not somewhere in the future—it is always and already here...truth can only be discovered in the aliveness of this moment. Love can only be experienced in this very heart, here and now. Awareness can only be realized as we discover the space and wakefulness of our own mind...our ultimate refuge is none other than our own being. There is a light of awareness that shines through each of us and guides us home. We are never separated from this luminous awareness, any more than waves are separated from ocean.

It is both simple and complex. How do we show up to the moments of this one life? What is our relationship to ourselves, others, and the world around us? How can we cultivate responsiveness, rather than reactivity, so that life happens with us and by us, rather than to us? At the end of our days, what will we remember most and be most grateful for? Where is the freedom and peace within this moment? One breath and each moment at a time.

**Reflect**

1. What does mindfulness mean to you?

2. To what extent do you see yourself continuing your mindfulness practice? What does it look like? How might you bring mindfulness into your daily life and activities?

3. Choose a mindfulness "buddy." Keep connected to your buddy and reach out when your practice needs a boost, to meditate and/or take classes together, to celebrate successes, or just to say hello.

4.  Activity: Choose a you in the future (one month, one year, three years from now, etc.). Write a letter to yourself about the things in mindfulness you want your future self to keep in mind. You can even submit it to www.futureme. org and they will email your letter to you at that point in the future.

*Helpful Guiding Questions*:

•   What type of lifestyle do you want to be living?
•   What values do you want to live by?
•   What will be important to keep in mind regarding presence, attention, communication, self-care, compassion, and taking time to pause?
•   What might you have forgotten by then that you want to remind yourself of?
•   What do you want to remember from that point onwards?

Dear Future Me:

# Bibliography

Brach, T. (2003). *True refuge: Finding peace and freedom in your own awakened heart.* New York: Bantam Press Books.

Hanh, T.N. (2011). *Your true home: The everyday wisdom of Thich Nhat Hanh.* Boulder: Shambhala.

# Resources

## A. Mindfulness Exam

*True/False*

1. Only certain people can be mindful.
2. Mindfulness involves clearing the mind and getting rid of unpleasant thoughts.
3. Mindfulness involves a willingness to be present with our experiences, thoughts, and emotions, whatever they may be.
4. Mindfulness is a passive and relaxing activity.
5. "What is my relationship to _____?" is a central question in mindfulness.
6. A Harvard study found that people spent only about fifty percent of their time in the present moment, and they were less happy when their mind was wandering, no matter where they were or what they were doing.
7. Studies suggest that mindfulness practice enhances the amygdala region of the brain.
8. Mindfulness research is still relatively new and emerging. More rigorous research methods and larger sample sizes are needed before declaring definitive outcomes.
9. Mindfulness is a skill that can grow with time and practice.
10. When working with thoughts in formal practice, it's best to stay on the train of thought until it's finished.
11. Through mindfulness, we can learn to cultivate gratitude, equanimity, and compassion.
12. Social psychologist and researcher James Pennebaker found that writing about stressful or traumatic events can help people process them and move forward.
13. Mindful technology use is not possible.
14. Active listening is not a part of mindful communication.
15. What you pay attention to is not in your control.

*Multiple Choice*

16. Mindfulness is a willingness to be present with openness and
    a)   Judgment.
    b)   Curiosity.
    c)   Harshness.
    d)   Clarity.
17. The T in the technique STOP stands for
    a)   Take a Breath.
    b)   Take it all in.
    c)   Take your anger out on someone.
    d)   Time yourself.
18. A beginner's mind means that we view our experiences as if
    a)   They were so easy even a beginner could try them.
    b)   They were as frustrating as they are for beginners.
    c)   They will never change.
    d)   They were happening for the first time.
19. Directed awareness through an anchor in practice
    a)   Can ground the mind when it is wandering.
    b)   Can help build concentration.
    c)   Can include the breath, body, sound, or a word/phrase.
    d)   All of the above.
20. Obstacles in practice include
    a)   Sleepiness.
    b)   Doubt.
    c)   Restlessness.
    d)   All of the above.
21. Equanimity means a
    a)   Groundedness and peace no matter the situation.
    b)   Willingness to change our circumstances.
    c)   Vitality for life.
    d)   Ability to see things for what we want them to be.
22. Attachment and aversion
    a)   Can show us where our work in acceptance is needed.
    b)   Can show us how to shape our lives the way we want them to be.
    c)   Should be followed for a path of less suffering.
    d)   Are always useful to base decisions on in life.
23. Types of formal practice include
    a)   Sitting meditation.
    b)   Walking meditation.
    c)   Mindful eating.
    d)   All of the above.

24. Strategies for working with thoughts include:
    a) Labeling thoughts.
    b) Acknowledging thoughts with a neutral phrase such as "thinking; thinking" or "thinking...and the sky is blue."
    c) Continually coming back to the breath or anchor.
    d) Visualization of thoughts passing like clouds in the sky.
    e) All of the above.
25. According to Martin Seligman, the 3 Ps that stunt recovery from setbacks include:
    a) Personalization, pervasiveness, permanence.
    b) Pervasiveness, purpose, puppies.
    c) Personalization, purpose, putting all our eggs in one basket.
    d) Playfulness, pettiness, permanence.
26. According to Barbara Fredrickson's broaden-and-build theory
    a) We can learn to broaden our thinking over time.
    b) When our mind is relaxed, we can see and create more possibilities.
    c) We can create a broad vision of our lives when we can see clearly.
    d) When we're stressed, our focus narrows and we can see clearly.
27. The A in the RAIN technique can stands for
    a) Altruism.
    b) Anchor.
    c) Allow.
    d) Anxiety.
28. When difficult emotions arise, with mindfulness we can choose to
    a) Become overwhelmed by them.
    b) Notice them and hold them with kindness and nonidentification.
    c) Use the RAIN technique.
    d) Both B and C.
29. Deactivating emotional reactivity involves
    a) Exploring how the emotion drives thinking.
    b) Finding space between the emotion, ourselves, and our response.
    c) Making sense of our emotions.
    d) Getting caught in the emotion.
30. Emotional granularity refers to
    a) Seeing the big picture behind the emotion.
    b) Labeling the nuance of an emotion.
    c) Examining the space between the emotion and ourselves.
    d) Exploring how the emotion is part of our identity.
31. Compassion is when difficulties are met with
    a) Kindness.
    b) Clarity.
    c) Lessons Learned.
    d) Hugs.

32. Self-compassion includes the elements of
    a) mindfulness and curiosity.
    b) mindfulness and judgment.
    c) mindfulness, kindness, shared humanity.
    d) mindfulness and hope.
33. Written Response: please answer the following questions in short paragraphs/a few sentences for each question.
    a) What does mindfulness mean to you?

    b) How has your practice evolved over the semester? How has your practice impacted you as it evolved?

    c) What are your next steps?

*ANSWERS*

1.  F
2.  F
3.  T
4.  F
5.  T
6.  T
7.  F
8.  T
9.  T
10. F
11. T
12. T
13. F
14. F
15. F
16. B
17. A
18. D
19. D
20. D
21. A
22. A
23. D
24. E
25. A
26. B
27. C
28. D
29. B
30. B
31. A (case can also be made for D)
32. C
33. Rubric criteria: thorough, reflective, demonstrates understanding and application of mindfulness principles and techniques.

## B. Guiding Questions for Complementary Reading

To enhance your understanding of mindfulness philosophy and application, read an additional book from the mindfulness field.

Recommended Options:

a.   *A Path with Heart* by Jack Kornfield
b.   *Insight Meditation* by Joseph Goldstein
c.   *Mindfulness in Plain English* by Bhante Gunaratana
d.   *Peace is Every Step* by Thich Nhat Hanh
e.   *The Mindful Path to Self-Compassion* by Christopher Germer
f.   *True Refuge* by Tara Brach
g.   *The Inner Work of Racial Justice* by Rhonda Magee

- Why did you choose your book?
- What do you hope to gain or learn from reading it?
- Choose a significant passage from your book. Why is it important? What does it mean to you?
- What are some of the emerging themes in your book? To what extent do they relate to your practice and life?
- What does the author suggest may be helpful in times of difficulty? In what way are these practices similar or different to what we have discussed in class thus far?
- Though the practices in this book are discussed in a secular framework, mindfulness has roots in Buddhist philosophy. To what extent does Buddhism inform the teachings of your author? What role does it play in their journey and teachings?
- Think of a current challenge you are going through or have gone through. Based on your understanding of the book thus far, how might the author suggest viewing or coping with it?
- If you could ask the author a question, what would it be?

## C. Student Panel: Mindfulness in the Classroom

As part of USC's USC Diversity, Equity, and Inclusion Week, six students (real names used) who completed the Introduction to Mindfulness course spoke about their experience. An excerpted transcript is included here. "Engaging in this open and honest conversation about mental health and mindfulness gave me so much hope for the future of college campuses and the ways in which they can choose to approach mental health," reflected panelist Jacqueline Berliner. "I am so proud to have been a part of this panel and I hope this event will prompt the start of an ongoing, open conversation about mental health on our campus which is essential and long overdue."

*Presentation*: "Mindfulness in the Classroom: Techniques for Situating Well-being Supports Alongside Academics for Inclusion and Equity in our Diverse Student Body," March 3, 2020.

*From left: moderator Linda Yaron Weston and undergraduates panelists Megan (Mae) Gates, Cristian Garcia, Drew Hodis, Jacqueline Berliner, Sudhakar Sood, Sahib Gill. Photograph by Julie Goler*

*Question 1: What would you say is the most significant way mindfulness has impacted you?*

*Mae:* "I would say I have two really big impacts that I took away from this course and just a mindfulness practice overall. The first is the power of perspective and the second would be experiencing my emotions and not becoming my emotions. These are two things I really had no idea about before I started practicing mindfulness. But now I fully understand the power of perspective with current situations. I think there is a really bad student culture across the board. Being young, especially when you are going into professions that require a lot of education, a lot of experience, everything just feels so detrimental. Like, if I fail this midterm, then I'm going to get a C in the class, then my GPA is going to be messed up, then I'm not going to get into grad school, then I'm going to be broke, then I'm not going to be able to pay my loans back. It just piles, and piles, and piles. And then we also have so many expectations from outside sources outside of ourselves. We feel like we owe something to our parents, we owe something to society, to ourselves, and these really small occurrences in our lives that really don't have a big impact at all seem the biggest and the worst things that ever happen to you.

Mindfulness has really allowed me to take rough patches, take hard days, hard weeks, failed midterms, failed exams, nearly failed classes, and not allow it to become a detriment to my life and the trajectory of my life. And I think if so many students had that with them, it would be a completely different world that we live in. And with mental health, I think that a lot of people struggle with depression and anxiety because we feel the weight of the world on our shoulders when we are extremely young, inexperienced, don't always have a lot of money, don't always have the most support in the world. It makes it really hard to navigate the day-to-day inconveniences. Luckily, now I am able to put so many more things into perspective and not jump to these horrible conclusions and recognize that even if I am having an overall rough semester that I am still very accomplished, I am still really empowered, and this is not something that is going to take away from my livelihood in the future.

Also, being able to experience emotions and recognize that that does not mean I am becoming that emotion. So for example, I've always struggled with depression and anxiety and I think before I was introduced to mindfulness it was like 'I am depressed,' 'I am anxious,' 'I am worried,' 'I am guilty.' But now I have a new perspective of 'well, I am experiencing depression' and I am not always depressed, I am not always anxious. And through my mindfulness practice and through therapy, and also just really filling my life with a lot of balance, I am able to recognize that we all have our highs and our lows and emotions come and go. There is very seldom ever consistent emotion and I think that really does help me cope with—and help me live with—some of the mental health issues that I have faced and kind of recognize that even though of course it sucks to feel this way, and it's not preferable that I feel this way, I am able to control my perspective and control my outlook on it to, at least, make it more bearable and make it something that I embrace, more so than something that I try to wash away and/or act like it is not there."

*Sahib:* "I feel like this class has given me a sort of vessel to navigate these hardships…It's helped me build that mind and body connection that I feel is so crucial. And personally, for my career, I know it's going to be very stressful. I have chosen a banking route and I'm going to be working really long hours and I actually feel like this class has helped me. I know I can't fully prepare for this, but I know it's helped me build that mental fortitude, while still expecting these emotions as they come and I do feel more comfortable now about the future than I did before, because it's always stressful. I'm sure we're all stressed out about our futures and I feel like a class like this does wonders and it's definitely the most memorable class I've had."

*Cristian:* "Similarly for me, I would say that discovering that USC offers this class honestly couldn't have come at a better time. The summer before taking this class is when I could say I first started experiencing symptoms of anxiety—to the point where it was interfering with my day-to-day life. Frankly, it was really scary. I thought about it obsessively. I was scared about how it would interfere not only with schoolwork, but also my interpersonal life to the point where it would definitely just cloud my thoughts. And that being said, this class definitely made me feel like I could regain control of my life. It reminded me that everything could fit in my head, not just anxiety. I don't need to identify with these adverse feelings. At the very least—I mean I still experience it on a day-to-day occasion— but at the very least, it reminded me that it doesn't need to control my life and that I have the tools to definitely make it more bearable and still find happiness and gratitude in my life."

*Drew:* "I had been in a state of trauma since the age of ten. For twelve years. I started working on it two years ago in therapy, trying to get out of it and a year and a half goes by and really nothing changed. Then I started taking your class in August of last year and in October I climbed out of the trauma. The first time in twelve years. I have been out since. There have been two times where I think I triggered it, but I just go on a bike ride and I'm better. I am just so grateful."

*Question 2: To what extent did having the course in your schedule alongside academic classes made a difference?*

*Jackie:* "I feel like having this class with all my other academics was really beneficial because I felt like all throughout high school and college, until taking this course, I felt like I was just trying to get my assignments in and I was just going through the motions. I wasn't really thinking about things that I like and things that were helping me. I used to work out all the time and I feel like it really helped me with my anxiety, but then I would come back to school and I would be like 'ok I don't have time' or I would just make up all these excuses. So, hav- ing this class and going through academics at the same time, it was kind of like a constant reminder to check in with myself and see what I needed, and it made space for self-care and reflection. By going through the semester intentionally making sure I was doing activities that helped me de-stress, like hanging out with friends, meditating, and working out, I was able to actually be more productive in my classes and just show up better in my relationships and my classes, and be less stressed overall. Basically, it just helped me create this habit of balance and showed me the power of having balance. That was always something that I always tried to have. I would always make that my New Year's resolution—I am going to have balance this semester—and it would go out the window in two weeks. Having this course and being accountable for mindfulness really helped create this habit for me. And now two semesters later, I definitely still have balance and it has been amazing and so helpful."

*Sahib:* "So, when I took this class, it was probably during my hardest semester. I was taking the full amount of units you could take and I had an internship I was balancing on the side and I could guarantee you that this was the class I looked forward to every single week because it made the semester so much easier. I can honestly say it was my favorite semester even though I was balancing so many things. I feel like it even built so many interpersonal skills. I was able to hang out with my friends more and actually cherish that time and be mindful while hanging out with them. It made it so much more enjoyable. In even any of Linda's classes (I've also taken Stress Management with her), I feel like you gain so many connections with people inside your classes. It's by far the most social class. You meet so many new people and you're all trying to be mindful–you're all just kind of going on this new journey. I was skeptical at first, but you know, I really felt like it made such a lasting impact on my semester."

*Mae:* "Going off of Jackie, I really like how you touched on how having it be an actual academic class holds you accountable. It's crazy how we will prioritize doing assignments and seeing people, going to events, going to work, but we won't prioritize what's best for ourselves. And I think it's great that I had this in a classroom environment because it held me accountable to taking care of myself and there is really no other environment that I could think of outside of therapy, that will actually hold you accountable to mindfulness. It's 100% self-driven and you have to hold yourself accountable, really, if it's going to be effective. And so, I think it was great. I was also taking nineteen units, three jobs, in sixty million different places at all times and it was great to have at least one time a week, two hours, knowing that I'm going to sit here and think about myself, and I'm going to build community, and I am going to earn academic credit for that, of course—but I'm also going to be held accountable for doing that through my classmates and my professor. And I think that's something that I now cherish so much now that I'm doing my practice alone because I don't have people asking me 'hey did you meditate this morning or tonight?' and 'did you do your reflection?' Luckily, I am now disciplined enough to know that is just what is really essential for me as an individual but I think it was a great environment to get exposed to mindfulness and having a community of people that are also in it with you makes it a lot easier to continue on that journey."

*Sudhakar:* "To build off that, most of the classes that I take are very science heavy, so we learn a lot of stuff—stuff about DNA and stuff like that. It's stuff that you don't, I mean it's important, but it's not really entailed to you. Whereas I feel like this course is really about personal growth and really would help you outside the classroom regardless of whatever field you are."

*Question 3: In our university context, to what extent has mindfulness impacted your academic learning?*

*Drew:* "So I have pretty severe ADHD—I'm sure you all saw me leave like half an hour in. It's because I can't sit in a chair for a half an hour. I don't take medication for it because I'm very sensitive to medication and so mindfulness is actually the thing that has helped me the most with my attention, focus, restlessness, anxiety—everything that goes with ADHD. And before I took the course and while I was taking the course, I never read anything for class, not a single page—sorry. I never turned anything in on time. I always had to beg my professors for forgiveness and to let me turn things in late. And I usually had a lot of difficulty paying attention in class. It was just the worst. But after this class, now I can sit in class and pay attention mostly, as long as I get up, and I've been turning in all my assignments in on time. I read the textbook for the first time probably since fifth grade the other day. I was pretty proud of myself. Mindfulness really, really helped me in my academics."

*Cristian:* "Similar for me, I mean school-related stress is something I'm pretty sure everyone in this room could definitely say they have experienced at one point of their lives. That's in addition to any other source of negativity or stress that people may have to deal with, and it could become a lot. And people may feel like there is a lot on their plate or too much in their head where they could actually focus on schoolwork. I am definitely the type of student who still gets pre-test jitters and whatnot, and if you throw coffee in the mix, that definitely exacerbates it.

For me, even as simple as just meditating before an exam. If I get anxious or stressed out while studying for an exam or cramming, then putting that time aside to just check in on myself and remind myself that I am capable. Holding these thoughts with kindness is always something that I have appreciated and that I actually got from this class. And I'm sure every other fellow panelist can attest to the fact that in our respective careers we will have to manage a lot of stress. And as a student who does eventually want to go to law school, I take notice of the fact that there are high rates of anxiety among lawyers and students in law school—and even the American Bar Association released several studies that show high rates of mental anguish amongst lawyers–so I do think it's something that is very beneficial and I'm definitely glad that there is more consciousness about the importance of mindfulness, not only daily practice, but in a workplace environment."

*Question 4: In our USC Diversity, Equity, and Inclusion week, can you speak to your experiences in how mindfulness has impacted you in any of these areas?*

*Sudhakar:* "I can speak to this, being a first-generation student and a transfer student from New York. I'd never been to California. Everyone told me that its very laid back and it's very different, but what I learned is that everyone experiences similar problems. I know coming in I dealt with imposter syndrome. And I am also a part of the Transfer Student Community, in which I overlook a program in which we pair incoming transfers with a mentor and so it's a common problem that all students, not just transfer students, deal with and just addressing the problem at first helps other people in general."

*Mae:* "I think for me, I have been extremely empowered to share the power of practicing good mental health and mindfulness in the Black community since I have taken Linda's mindfulness course. I think that across the board we have a huge disparity with mental health and mindfulness in the Black community. There are so many conversations that are never held. Growing up and being raised, my parents never necessarily talked to me about mental health. They never coached me on what does mental health mean, how to take care of yourself mentally and emotionally, how can we as your parents be supportive to you in the community. And just through my own practices, through therapy and my practices through mindfulness, I have learned so much about myself. During the time I was taking the course, actually I was co-executive director of the Black Student Assembly here on campus, and I did everything I could to bring mindfulness into my leadership in the Black community because Black students here on campus face so many adversities that so many people do not understand. When we go back to our own communities, even when I go home for break, there are so many conversations that we can't have with our families, we can't have with our parents. We can't have an honest conversation about the mental effects of being a college student.

And so, through this course, now that I have a really strong foundation and understanding of mindfulness, and also through my own practices of therapy, I have been really proactive within my leadership in the Black community to ensure that I am having honest conversations with all of my peers, faculty, and professionals I work with, about mental health in the Black community and how we can strengthen it, how we can make it a really integral part on the impact that we have here on campus. I recently became a member of Alpha Kappa Alpha incorporated. It's the first Black sorority. And through that, we have a lot of conversations among ourselves as Black women. What does mental health mean to us? What are the disparities that we had growing up? And how can we ensure that this becomes an integral conversation in our community and every part of life that we walk through? Whether it's work, school, social—how can we introduce these conversations? How can we share our knowledge about mindfulness and mental health to kind of really start reversing intergenerational trauma? I have done a lot of research on it, and luckily Linda has sent me some things as well, but essentially a lot of the experts are now saying that mindfulness is key in the reversal and stopping of intergenerational trauma in Black communities. And so, it's really about learning how do we get Black adolescents, all the way to the elderly, interested and knowledgeable about mindfulness and therapy, ensuring that we use it as a tool to really cure traumas, but also play more integral roles in all the communities we are in."

*(Audience) Question 5: I wanted to ask Sahib—you said you were skeptical going in. Can you tell me a little bit about why you went ahead and took the class anyways?*

*Sahib:* "Yeah, so as I mentioned before, I had a really tough semester before, and so I was really interested in researching classes that would help me with my mental health, so that's why I took both Stress Management and Mindfulness with Linda that next semester. And at first, it's hard, you know. I was still skeptical the first couple of weeks. The very first day of class we meditated, and it was something I have never done before and I found my mind going all over the place. I had so much trouble focusing on being in the moment and I think just like learning how to shoot a basketball, it's something you practice every day and you get good at. And I found that the better I got at my practice, the less skeptical I was and happier I was overall and it's just something I had to practice and really get in touch with. I think it was actually putting myself in a position that made myself practice this mindfulness and actually give it a chance so that it could actually help me out in the long run."

*(Audience) Question 6: Do you have a community that you can continue to engage with after the class is over? And, if you don't, and wanted one, what would that look like?*

*Jackie:* "I feel like the course was a really good community builder. I took it two semesters and I feel that in both of them everyone was very open and spoke about everything that they were feeling and I felt that it was cool to see that other people were going through exactly the same thing you were going through, or like you've gone through before, or just anything like that. So that was a really good aspect out of it, and then I feel like coming out of the course I did want more of that community, like speaking about mindfulness, or practicing it. Right now, I'm actually taking a performance science class at USC and it's all about the science of gratitude and mindfulness, and I also took a creativity class which is all about that. So I feel that I have been able to find other ways to like bring that mindfulness into my life with community, but I also attend yoga classes because I also feel that's a really good community and I feel like I really find it in yoga."

*Sudhakar:* "Going off of what Jackie said, I think that once you get more comfortable with mindfulness, you realize, that everyone has these problems, and whoever you talk to, you kind of break that barrier and you go below the surface level. And then you realize you guys all have the same stressors. It kind of builds that genuine relationship—that connection. It doesn't have to be a support group, but just realizing that you're actually having real conversations and going below the surface level—it helps."

*(Audience) Question 7: If it's not a class, if you had free drop-in sessions, would you go to them? Like 15 minutes, 30 minutes, maybe an hour—would you go to them? Or did it spark because it was a part of the curriculum?*

*Cristian:* "I mean I would definitely say the curriculum sparked my interest in mindfulness and I would definitely just say the hardest thing would be it conflicting with the schedule. If it were just offered during a time where we didn't have class or maybe extracurriculars, yeah, I would definitely still go to these sessions. It's always nice to engage in the practice with other people, friends, I do think it builds that sense of community. As we mentioned earlier, it cultivates that place where it feels ok to be vulnerable in. I mean it's nice seeing other people, and you know it lets you know that whatever you're feeling is ok, and that other people could relate and help you through it."

*Sudhakar:* "I think maybe as an outsider, never practicing mindfulness, it might be intimidating and daunting, but I think if you are able to get people, and break that barrier, I know I would definitely stop by. I think the challenge with that is breaking the barrier because we aren't taught this stuff in school, so I guess that's the whole purpose of this—educating the other people and letting them know how important this is– and this should be just as important as our GE's or whatever we take, because we don't really cultivate this personal growth sense in our education."

*(Audience) Question 8: As an academic program, would you have liked to have seen this in high school, in elementary school? When do you think you could have started doing mindfulness? I am curious about how you could talk to a high school group.*

*Sahib:* "Personally for me, as I mentioned earlier about my high school, it was definitely a stressful time. I think that if we at least embedded these ideas—just the concept of mindfulness into our heads at an earlier age. High school is good.

I think we definitely need it there. Kids are under so much stress. They're all hormonal, they don't have any idea of what's going on—so many tests they have to take, college apps. That is definitely a time where they should have these ideas."

*Cristian:* "I mean for me, I would just reassure them that what they are experiencing doesn't have to be something that is necessarily a sense of shame. Being open about your emotions, letting people know that you aren't feeling 100%, is something that is ok. I can definitely relate to that. In high school, I didn't really see mindfulness as something that was or would be really important in my life or play a huge role in my life, whatever reason that maybe. But I do think that reminding high school students, frankly especially high school boys, that it is ok to be emotional and go through some things, and especially talk about it."

*Mae:* "I would say as early as possible, like kindergarten. I have a little cousin. She is at a phenomenal private school and they teach little kids to meditate. I don't know how they get them to sit down, but I was home for the holidays, and she had an outburst over something and she went in the corner and sat—and it was crazy. So I was talking to her mom, where did she learn to do that? *I* just learned how to do that. They do little meditations with the kids in the school, and I think that it is so important because I'm twenty-one now and when I first started therapy and mindfulness—there is so much, even today, unlearning and undoing I have to do because I was just not taught the correct way to handle my emotions and conflict management. I have these horrible things and ways I handle conflict and emotion that I really had to unlearn to do. I'm still unlearning them. And it is really hard to break a cycle of how you deal with emotion and conflict. And so, if I ever have kids, I promise you, straight out the womb, I am going to try to really instill in them a good relationship with their emotions and a great way to handle conflict with anyone.

I would definitely say in high school. It's really hard, but also really important. I think high school is the first time you are actually aware of your emotions, aware of depression, anxiety, and hardships that you go through. There are a lot of high schoolers, I know I felt like this in high school, who really feel like they don't have anyone to talk to—because you damn sure can't tell your parents half the things that you are doing, and because you can't tell them what you're actually doing, you can't really be honest with them about how you're feeling. I think that high schoolers love examples. Like I used always look up to people who would lead by example. So for example, if you do want them to get more in touch with mindfulness and their emotions, be open and honest with them about your experiences in high school and young adulthood, and how you got through them. They need something to relate to, because unfortunately you still have negative stigmas around mental health and mistakes that you make as a young adult and by having someone that is honest about their experiences, I think that could really help them open up and actually lean into the practice."

## D. Course Design and Pedagogy

The Introduction to Mindfulness course I developed at USC is comprised of five modules: principles of mindfulness, and mindfulness as it relates to body, emotions, thoughts, and daily life. Students complete the course workbook and read a book from the mindfulness field to deepen knowledge of practice and theory. They choose a group area of daily life to incorporate mindfulness into—which provides an opportunity to build relationships and have a supportive sub-group within the classroom community. To be exposed to a variety of styles and perspectives, students hear from classroom guest speakers and take meditation classes of their choice outside our class. Assessments include the group presentation, an exam, module reflection forms, and a final reflection.

### *Benefits of Mindfulness as a For-Credit Course*

1. *Built-in academic schedule*: It contextualizes self-care and mental health within a student's school day. This is not something that is an extra outside activity or something to do in spare, time, but rather it situates mental health and well-being within the schedule. Schools typically offer multiple types of mental health supports for students, including counseling or workshops—and while they have much value, not all students are inclined to seek them out and may not be consistent in accessing resources when needed. Having a class built into their schedule alongside academic courses provides each enrolled student with a consistent practice in self-care for over a duration of time.
2. *Peer group identification*: Peer group similarity of a for-credit course creates a sense of safety and belonging for students to feel comfortable with others who are in a similar place in life and experiencing common challenges. This builds community, social connection, and relationships, which are powerful elements of well-being that support mental and social health. "In class she has you break into groups about self-care and all that stuff," remarked Lana, a junior majoring in cinematic arts, in an interview about the course. "I did relationships, so we're really focusing on listening to others, so, I would say the class has really helped. It's also just provided me with a group of people who really care about loving people and building relationships—so that's been great because that's when we can really talk about it together as a group."
3. *Accountability*: Because students sign up within their course schedule and are assigned a grade, they are more inclined to complete the full duration of the course and fully participate in the experience. Such courses not prone to the same kind of community class attrition.
4. *Length for depth*: Our semester is fifteen weeks long. This period of in-depth practice and community building means more practice time and deeper understanding and application.

### *Tips on Using This Book Across Disciplines*

1.  Relevant sections can be incorporated into thematic units across subject areas. For example, section 4.2 Resilience might be used in a unit on overcoming obstacles or section 4.3 Identity and Social Consciousness might be used in a unit on social justice or civic engagement.
2.  Relevant sections can be used within an advisory, life skills, or health curriculum, particularly: 1.4 Mindful Learning, 2.4 Healthy Living, 4.3 Identity and Social Consciousness, 5.2 Decision Making, and 5.4 Success and Careers.
3.  Quote analysis of primary source passages can be used to increase critical thinking and literacy skills. Students can analyze quotations from mindfulness, history, philosophy, and literature that are incorporated throughout the book.
4.  Extended study of poetry or ted talks included in the "Reflect" sections at the end of each module can deepen understanding and relevance of topics.
5.  Taking a few minutes to start and end each class with a few breaths to pause can help set the tone for class and prepare the mind and body for learning.
6.  Explicitly teaching tools for students to navigate difficult emotions can aid in being more responsive and less reactive in life and the classroom.

### *Pedagogy and Principles of Classroom Teaching*

I've found the following principles of classroom teaching to be helpful in creating a safe, relevant, and meaningful student experience. They are reflective of my experience teaching high school and university academic and well-being courses.

1.  *Purpose*: it is important to know the purpose of why you teach, what learning objectives students will achieve, and what classroom conditions can help students meet those goals. Ideally, goals align with instructional content, methods, and assessment. Learning objectives are the goals students achieve through the experiences created in the course. Outline a beginning, middle, end (into, through, beyond) of class activities with a timeline that will help achieve learning goals. Budget time to spend the most time on the most important things. Students need to know their purpose in learning the content and why it's important. Guiding Question: what is your mission statement and philosophy of teaching?
2.  *Conditions for Learning*: more than explicitly teaching anyone anything, intentional teaching creates the conditions for learning to occur. An exploration of the conditions for learning can help create systems, structures, and class environments for learning to happen when students feel safe and supported and have the tools they need to learn. Guiding Questions: what are the conditions for learning in your classroom? What are the biggest strengths and challenges in your classroom?

3.  *Relationships and Investment*: we are teaching people, not subject areas. Building relationships with students helps create trust, investment, and a culture of caring. Structure opportunities for small and whole group discussion, as well as group projects to help students build relationships with each other. Guiding Questions: what do relationships look like in your classroom (teacher to student and student to student)? What does investment and engagement in a student-centered classroom mean and look like?

4.  *Active Learning*: in active learning (versus passive learning) classrooms, students are engaged in the subject and apply their knowledge. Look at the actions students are doing to measure this—asking questions, reflecting, discussing, writing, speaking, etc. This is the difference between a student-centered or teacher-centered classroom. Guiding Questions: what does active learning mean and look like in the classroom? What are students doing in a class they have investment and ownership in?

5.  *Growth Model Differentiation*: one of the biggest challenges in a classroom is how to make a course equally rigorous for students who are all at different skill levels. Differentiating instruction entails reframing what we are instructing and approaching learning from a skills-based lens. The challenge is not to get everyone at the same level; it's how to maximally increase everyone's skills individually through a shared learning experience. In this sense, the role of teacher transforms to one of a coach who creates experiences for students to help them reach their highest potential outcome. Guiding Questions: how do you define high expectations? What do they look like in a differentiated learning classroom?

6.  *Equity and Access*: each student may have different learning styles or needs. Clear structure and consistent boundaries help establish fair policies for all students. Equity of student voice in the classroom can be fostered through structured discussion. Guiding questions can help facilitate that discussion. Normalizing student experiences and creating a culturally responsive, inclusive classroom will help students feel safe and heard. Guiding Question: what does equity and access mean and look like in the classroom?

7.  *Social Justice*: how can classrooms be equitable and humane spaces that honor the diversity of individual backgrounds? Create a safe space for students to explore culturally relevant topics including race, class, and gender. Discuss inequities, stereotypes, privilege, democracy, and freedom as it relates to individuals, groups, and society. Be an advocate and ally for students and teach a curriculum that reflects their struggles and hopes. Guiding Question: what does social justice mean and look like in the classroom?

8.  *Trauma-sensitive*: each student enters the classroom with their own challenges and experiences. In the midst of this, what will it take for each one to feel safe, heard, and understood? How can we teach skills of resilience, emotional regulation, and processing difficult experiences? Acknowledge challenges and create space to talk about them. Begin with a few breaths

to start and end class. Build supportive relationships with students and give them opportunities to develop them with each other. Guiding Question: how might student challenges impact their learning and class experience?

9. *Assessment*: how will you know students have learned what you wanted them to learn? Formative (along the way checks for understanding) and summative (final application of knowledge) assessments will measure if students have achieved learning goals. Use formative assessment data to inform instruction. Guiding Questions: what formative and summative assessment processes are in place in your classroom? Chart in three columns your goals, instructional learning experiences, and assessment to cross-check alignment.

10. *Collaborative Professional Growth:* like anything, teaching is a skill that grows with practice. Colleagues can help us more clearly see what is happening in our classrooms, reflect together, and share strategies for what works. Peer review or Critical Friends protocols and practices can be helpful here, with "critical" in this sense referring to how others are vital and important to our own learning. Below is a sample protocol for debriefing classroom observations in a relational mindfulness framework. Guiding Question: what is my relationship to collaboration and feedback?

*Peer Review Classroom Observation Protocol: Noticing*

*Purpose:* to neutrally share what was noticed in a classroom observation. The protocol creates a structure for discussing what occurred in the classroom in a neutral, nonjudgmental framework.

*Focus Area:* before observation, instructor shares which focus area that they would like another set of eyes for. Example: student discourse.

*Observation Time*: 15-20 minutes. Debrief within a few days following observation.

*Setting Intentions:* before debriefing, it is recommended that each set an intention for the protocol. Example: to objectively share what was noticed or to openly receive what was noticed.

*Protocol Norms:*
- Sharing and receiving from a place of curiosity, nonjudgment, caring, and openness
- Be kind, specific, and helpful
- Focused on student learning
- Growth mindset
- Assume best intentions

*Protocol*: Repeated question: "What did you notice?"

Observer asks instructor, "What did you notice?" After response, observer says, "Thank you" and repeats question, "What did you notice?" This continues for four minutes. After that time, the roles switch and, for four minutes, instructor asks observer, "What did you notice?" and replies, "Thank you." The "thank you" is an appreciation of what was noticed and shared. Pause for a few breaths before and after each person shares. Script:

*Observer:* "What did you notice?"
*Instructor:* Answers something they noticed about the class lesson.
*Observer:* "Thank you. What did you notice?"
   Repeated for four minutes.
   Thank each other for participation.


Roles switch.


*Instructor:* "What did you notice?"
*Observer:* Answers something they noticed about the class lesson.
*Instructor:* "Thank you. What did you notice?"
   Repeated for four minutes.
   Thank each other for participation.

Two-minute debrief each on how the process went, key takeaways, and next steps (Instructor chooses order).

*Tips*:

- Try to avoid statements that interpret or classify what happened and what was thought about it and focus on *what* happened.
- Focus on what students are doing, rather than what instructor is doing. Share statements of what happened in the class rather than "you" statements.
- Throughout, participants can notice any emotions, thoughts, or sensations that may arise in them as they both share and receive what was noticed.
- Variation: can repeat the question "What did you wonder?" to generate curiosity and prompt reflection.

## E. Resources for Further Study

### Select Apps

- UCLA Mindful: https://www.uclahealth.org/marc
- Mindful USC: https://mindful.usc.edu
- Insight Timer: https://insighttimer.com
- Calm: https://www.calm.com
- Headspace: https://www.headspace.com
- 10% Happier: https://www.tenpercent.com

### Select Retreat Centers

- Spirit Rock: https://www.spiritrock.org
- Insight Meditation Society: https://www.dharma.org
- Shambala Mountain Center: https://www.shambhalamountain.org
- Vallecitos Mountain Retreat Center: https://www.vallecitos.org
- Inward Bound: https://ibme.info/programs/youth/

### Recommended Books

Foundations of Mindfulness

1. *Full Catastrophe Living,* Jon Kabat-Zinn
2. *Fully Present: The Art, Science, and Power of Mindfulness,* Diana Winston and Susan Smalley
3. *A Heart as Wide as the World: Living with Mindfulness, Wisdom, and Compassion,* Sharon Salzberg
4. *How to Meditate: A Practical Guide to Making Friends with Your Mind,* Pema Chödrön
5. *Mindfulness: A Practical Guide to Awakening,* Joseph Goldstein
6. *Mindfulness in Plain English,* Bhante Gunaratana
7. *The Miracle of Mindfulness: An Introduction to the Practice of Meditation,* Thich Nhat Hanh
8. *Natural Wakefulness: Discovering the Wisdom We Were Born With,* Gaylon Ferguson
9. *Wherever You Go, There You Are: Mindfulness Meditation in Everyday Life,* Jon Kabat-Zinn
10. *Zen Mind, Beginners Mind: Informal Talks on Zen Meditation and Practice,* Shunryu Suzuki

Deepening Practice in Mindfulness

11. *Being Black: Zen and the Art of Living with Fearlessness and Grace*, angel Kyodo williams
12. *How to Train a Wild Elephant and Other Adventures in Mindfulness*, Jan Chozen Bays
13. *Insight Meditation: The Practice of Freedom*, Joseph Goldstein
14. *The Meditations*, Marcus Aurelius
15. *No Mud, No Lotus: The Art of Transforming Suffering*, Thich Nhat Hanh
16. *A Path with Heart: A Guide Through the Perils and Promises of Spiritual Life*, Jack Kornfield
17. *Peace is Every Step: The Path of Mindfulness in Everyday Life*, Thich Nhat Hanh
18. *Radical Acceptance: Embracing your Life with the Heart of the Buddha*, Tara Brach
19. *True Refuge: Finding Peace and Freedom in Your Own Awakened Heart*, Tara Brach
20. *The Wise Heart: A Guide to the Universal Teachings of Buddhist Psychology*, Jack Kornfield

Applications of Mindfulness

21. *The Body Keeps Score: Brain, Mind, and Body in the Healing of Trauma*, Bessel Van der Kolk
22. *Daring Greatly: How the Courage to Be Vulnerable Transforms the Way We Live, Love, Parent, and Lead*, Brene Brown
23. *The Inner Work of Racial Justice: Healing Ourselves and Transforming our Communities through Mindfulness*, Rhonda Magee
24. *Mindful of Race: Transforming Racism From the Inside Out*, Ruth King
25. *Mindsight: The New Science of Personal Transformation*, Daniel Siegel
26. *Radical Dharma: Talking Race, Love, and Liberation*, angel Kyodo williams, Lama Rod Owens, Jasmine Syedullah
27. *The Mindful Path to Self-Compassion: Freeing Yourself from Destructive Thoughts and Emotions*, Christopher Germer
28. *The Telomere Effect: A Revolutionary Approach to Living Younger, Healthier, Longer*, Elissa Epel and Elizabeth Blackburn
29. *The Upside of Stress: Why Stress Is Good for You, and How to Get Good at It*, Kelly McGonigal
30. *You Belong: A Call for Connection*, Sebene Selassie

*Teaching Mindfulness*

31. *A Clinician's Guide to Teaching Mindfulness: The Comprehensive Session-by Session Program for Mental Health Professionals and Health Care Providers*, Cristiane Wolf and Greg Sherpa, et al.
32. *Mindful Games Activity Cards: 55 Fun Ways to Share Mindfulness with Teens and Kids*, Susan Kaiser Greenland and Annaka Harris
33. *The Mindful Schools Curriculum for Adolescents: Tools for Developing Awareness*, Oren Jay Sofer and Matthew Brensilver
34. *Teaching Mindfulness to Empower Adolescents*, Matthew Brensilver, JoAnna Hardy, Oren Jay Sofer
35. *The Self-Compassion Workbook for Teens: Mindfulness and Compassion Skills to Overcome Self-Criticism and Embrace Who You Are*, Karen Bluth
36. *The Whole-Brain Child: 12 Revolutionary Strategies to Nurture your Child's Developing Mind, Survive Everyday Parenting Struggles, and Help your Family Thrive*, Dan Siegal

# Index